Classic Restaurants
OF
DES MOINES
AND Their Recipes

D1569671

Classic Restaurants

OF

DES MOINES

AND *Their Recipes*

DARCY DOUGHERTY MAULSBY

AMERICAN PALATE

Published by American Palate
A Division of The History Press
Charleston, SC
www.historypress.com

Copyright © 2020 by Darcy Dougherty Maulsby
All rights reserved

Cover images: Des Moines's dining scene has included an array of beloved restaurants through the years, including (*clockwise from top left*) Bamie's Pizza House, Lonnie's Drive-In, Stella's Blue Sky Diner and Porky's Diner.

First published 2020

Manufactured in the United States

ISBN 9781467145459

Library of Congress Control Number: 2020941804

Notice: The information in this book is true and complete to the best of our knowledge. It is offered without guarantee on the part of the author or The History Press. The author and The History Press disclaim all liability in connection with the use of this book.

Contents

Acknowledgements

I t has been said that history gives answers only to those who know how to ask questions. I knew asking the right questions of the right people would be essential to tell the stories of the classic restaurants of Des Moines accurately. Fortunately, a lot of wonderful people said yes when I reached out to request an interview, tour a museum, sit down to a meal or visit at the bar to hear stories of days gone by.

Thanks to Lew Bolton, president of Bolton & Hay, for letting me peek into the archives of one hundred years of Des Moines restaurant history.

I can't tell you how much I appreciate food historian, Des Moines native and chef extraordinaire George Formaro for caring enough about Des Moines's culinary history to keep the stories and flavors alive through his restaurants; his fun, uplifting Facebook posts; and his willingness to make time for a face-to-face interview with me at the Gateway Market in Des Moines.

Then there's the energetic, charming Patricia Civitate ("Mrs. C"), director of the Italian-American Cultural Center of Iowa, who has done an amazing job with her museum volunteers showcasing Des Moines's incredible Italian restaurant heritage. Speaking of Italian, I owe a big thank-you to Ron and Ann Bonanno. Not only did they welcome me into their West Des Moines home on a cold, snowy, icy November day to share stories of Ron's beloved father, Frank, who ran Bamie's Pizza House, but they also made me an authentic Bamie's pizza—truly a wonderful, memorable experience!

I'll also never forget that Saturday afternoon on a chilly, sunny November 2019 day when I walked into the Hy-Vee Market Grille in Johnston to meet Stanley Griffin Jr. Thank you, Stan, for giving me an insider's look into the ways racism reared its ugly head in Des Moines but was fearlessly challenged by your mother, Edna, and brave people like her.

While writing and researching can be a lonely process at times, it has also been a joy to connect with fellow history buffs at the Fort Des Moines Museum, those who knew Des Moines's dinner theater scene well (Gary Propstein, Tom Milligan and John Busbee) and those who have been around Des Moines long enough to experience (and often guide) the changes not only in the dining scene but also the city itself. They include Van Harden at WHO Radio, publisher and entrepreneur Connie Wimer, Chef Lisa LaValle, food writer Jim Duncan, real estate developer and restaurateur Bruce Gerleman, hotel owner Bob Conley, Tursi's Latin King owner Bob Tursi, Exile Brewing Company owner R.J. Tursi and Chuck's Restaurant owner Emily Jones.

Finally, I'm grateful for the talented team at The History Press, including my acquisitions editor, Chad Rhoad, who are committed to preserving local history and helped make this book a reality. They understand what author Pearl Buck meant when she wrote, "If you want to understand today, you have to search yesterday."

Introduction

When my editor asked me if I'd be willing to submit a proposal for the book you now hold in your hands, my first instinct was to say no. It's not that I didn't like the topic—I loved it. I knew that a book like this could add a unique twist to preserving local history. I just didn't think I was the right person to write it.

I'm a farm girl from Lake City, a small town two hours northwest of Des Moines. I've never worked in a restaurant. While I'm an avid home cook, I'm not a professionally trained chef. What I did have going for me is that I'm a native Iowan who has lived in this state most of my life. I've made many trips to Des Moines, starting in the 1980s with high school basketball tournaments, state science fair competitions and state FFA conventions in my school days. I lived in the Des Moines metro area for six years after college and loved to explore all areas of the city. Through it all, you've got to eat, right?

That fit well with my role as an ag journalist, since I essentially write about food for a living. As I began interviewing current and former Des Moines–area restaurant owners and their descendants, I realized quickly that farmers and restaurateurs have a lot in common. Like farmers, many restaurateurs are independent business owners. They are hardworking, family-oriented people who care about their local community. They want to grow their future here in Iowa and leave a legacy of success.

Restaurant owners, like farmers, also have had to adapt to changing times. These changes affect the people they serve. As I looked back on the places I used to enjoy, like the Younkers Tea Room downtown, I realized that I, too, had experienced part of Des Moines's classic restaurants. I knew that these were stories worth sharing.

I'm humbled to have the opportunity to document much of this history through *Classic Restaurants of Des Moines and Their Recipes*. While there's no way I could include every restaurant, this book helps capture the flavor that distinguishes not only Des Moines but also the history of Iowa. In case you're wondering, the restaurants selected for this book were based on a variety of factors, including how many times they appeared on polls and informal lists of beloved classic restaurants of Des Moines, how long they were in business, whether anyone who owned the business is still available for an interview, whether there were many stories of the restaurant in the local or national press and whether there were high-quality photos or other illustrations available.

Pull up a chair and let's dig in. These stories, like a satisfying meal, are best when shared.

CHAPTER I

Midwestern Roots Mixed with Ethnic Accents

In some ways, the restaurant heritage of Des Moines is a fairly recent phenomenon. While the history of Des Moines dates to the early 1840s (back when the area was known as Fort Des Moines), restaurants weren't a big part of the economic and cultural landscape of the city until the early twentieth century.

Although the Iowa General Assembly chose Des Moines in 1857 as the state's new capital, the city grew slowly. The outbreak of the Civil War in 1861 slowed western migration. Attempts to run steamboat traffic up the Des Moines River to the new capital city met with limited success. Dry goods had to be brought in by horse-drawn wagons until well after the Civil War. Iowa's more established cities along the Mississippi River continued to be larger population centers than Des Moines.

While agriculture remained an economic driver, insurance companies were beginning to create a booming business sector in Des Moines by the latter part of the nineteenth century. More milestones included the founding of Drake University in 1881 and the completion of Iowa's state capitol in 1886.

Still, Des Moines was hardly a major metropolitan area. By 1880, the census counted 22,408 residents. Up to this point, there were many more beer breweries in early Des Moines than restaurants, noted Chef George Formaro, who was raised in an Italian family on the east side of Des Moines.

While Des Moines's population jumped to 50,093, according to the 1890 census, the city was tiny compared to New York City, with more than

1.5 million residents at the time, or Chicago, which boasted nearly 1.1 million residents by 1890. Still, there were enough people to support the growth of restaurants in Des Moines.

"There were a lot of workingmen's cafés in Des Moines back in the day," explained Formaro, the visionary behind some of Des Moines's most successful eateries, including Centro, Django, South Union Bread Café, Gateway Market & Café, Malo and Zombie Burger + Drink Lab. "Their menus were very similar, with sandwiches and basic entrées."

KING YING LOW OFFERED A TASTE OF THE EXOTIC

It seems almost improbable today, but Des Moines's longest-lived restaurant wasn't focused on midwestern meat-and-potatoes fare. It was King Ying Low, which began serving Chinese-inspired dishes in the early 1900s. Seriously? Oh yes. It turns out the residents of Des Moines more than a century ago were more than willing to indulge in one of the hottest culinary trends sweeping the nation: the chop suey house. "That was a flavor explosion compared to what most people at the time were used to," Formaro said. "It was irresistible."

The story began far from Des Moines in the 1840s, when the first mass migrations of people from China began to land in North America, mostly to work in the California Gold Rush. While Chinatowns began to spring up from West Coast cities to New York in subsequent years, most people outside these neighborhoods drew the line at eating in Chinese restaurants. "Who knew what floated in their incomprehensible stews," noted "Mixed Bits: The True History of Chop Suey," which appeared on AmericanHeritage.com in 2017.

As word slowly got out about how delicious, novel and affordable Chinese food could be, however, adventurous eaters were drawn to Chinatowns in America's big cities. "They visited usually as part of 'slumming' parties, looking for outlandish scenes, a whiff of danger and chop suey," added the article.

Chop suey got its biggest boost when Li Hung Chang, a Chinese ambassador, made a highly ballyhooed official visit to the United States in August 1896. When he landed in New York, every local paper filled its pages with details about the city's distinguished guest, from his exotic dress to his opinion on whether women should ride bicycles. Reporters from

William Randolph Hearst's *New York Journal* were particularly interested in what Li Hung Chang ate.

Legend has it that while the ambassador was visiting New York City, his cooks invented a dish composed of celery, bean sprouts and meat in a tasty sauce to serve his American guests. The dish was supposedly created to satisfy both Chinese and American tastes. Whether or not the tale is entirely true, Li Hung Chang definitely influenced the creation of chop suey.

In the wake of his visit, everything Chinese was the rage. As Chinese food moved out of Chinatown in metropolitan areas like New York and into small cities as distant as Des Moines, restaurant owners altered the dishes to conform to the tastes of their new customers.

When King Ying Low debuted in Des Moines around 1907, it likely created a sensation among diners who may have been bored with "the insipidity of cheap chophouses and the sameness of [most] restaurants," in the words of "Mixed Bits." In an era of change and expansion, people wanted to try something alien and exciting, and chop suey—made with exotic ingredients like bean sprouts, water chestnuts and soy sauce—fit the bill perfectly. The dish was also filling, easy to make in bulk and inexpensive, making it attractive to a range of people, as it became a standard part of the urban diet.

Within a few years of King Ying Low's debut, the restaurant was cited in a full-page advertisement for the sixtieth-anniversary celebration of Brinsmaids, a foodservice supply company in Des Moines. The ad, which appeared in the April 16, 1914 edition of the *Des Moines Tribune*, noted that Brinsmaids had been in business in Des Moines since 1854 and continued to be the foodservice supplier of choice for the leading hotels, clubs, restaurants and soda fountains in Des Moines and across Iowa.

During the sixtieth-anniversary specials, customers could get etched ice tea glasses for $1.75 per dozen (about $45 in today's dollars), along with popular Blue Bird china dinner plates on sale for $4.80 per dozen (nearly $125 today). The bottom of the ad also offers an intriguing glimpse into the restaurant and foodservice world of Des Moines in 1914. The list of Brinsmaids' sixty-eight featured customers included King Ying Low, along with some other names that are still familiar today, including the Savery Hotel, *Successful Farming* magazine, Iowa Methodist Hospital, Iowa Lutheran Hospital and Mercy Hospital.

King Ying Low made the news again on April 8, 1924, when a front-page headline in the *Des Moines Evening Tribune* proclaimed "King Ying Low, Des Moines' Oldest Chop Suey, Passes into New Hands." "Lee Din is going home," the article stated. "For 22 years, he has stood at his desk at the King Ying Low restaurant now at Seventh and Mulberry Streets, nodding courteously to the stream of guests who sauntered in and out. Nimbly, Lee's fingers have shifted the wooden spheres on the ebony counting board, the device which antedated the modern adding machine by 5,000 years, and has totaled swiftly and silently the checks of the almost endless que [*sic*] of patrons—judges, physicians, businessmen, newspaper folk and actors."

The article noted the "hungry, happy crowds" who patronized King Ying Low, dining at the restaurant's marble-topped tables. "There are streaks of gray in the black hair of Lee Din," the article continued, "and around his genial eyes are the tiny lines that tell of the years or of smiles, or of both. It has been long since Lee saw the land of his fathers, and year by year the desire has been growing to see China."

Lee Din had come to America in 1880, shortly before the Chinese Exclusion Act of 1882, which was the first significant law restricting immigration into the United States. This law suspended Chinese immigration for ten years and declared Chinese immigrants ineligible for naturalization.

Din worked for importing companies on the Pacific coast before relocating to Minnesota, where he worked in the import business in Minneapolis/St. Paul. "One day a fellow countryman came into his store. 'There would be money in a good restaurant in Des Moines if the food was good, prices low and everything clean,' he told Lee. 'Des Moines people are good people with whom to deal.'"

A few months later, Lee opened Iowa's first chop suey restaurant at the Palm Garden Café at Fifth and Locust Streets. It was crowded with customers from the first noon lunch. "The guests ate up all the food that had been purchased for the entire day for that meal. People continued to throng, and by and by the restaurant would no longer hold all who would come," the *Tribune* said.

Lee moved and expanded his popular restaurant twice, both times on Mulberry Street, as the business continued to grow. By the time he was running King Ying Low at Seventh and Mulberry, his restaurant staff included Quong Lee and Lee Ban.

Now a grandfather with high school–aged grandchildren, Lee Din was preparing to leave Des Moines on May 5, 1924, with his family and go to China. "Good management, clean food and thick steaks served at a net profit of 1 cent each have made it possible," noted the *Tribune*.

The article reminisced about the changes Lee Din had seen during his time in Des Moines and indicated what a beloved community member he'd

When King Ying Low debuted in Des Moines around 1907, it was part of the chop suey craze sweeping America. The restaurant lasted nearly one hundred years in downtown Des Moines. *Author's collection.*

become. "The young bloods who used to roll up to Lee's place in hacks [horse-drawn cabs] are middle-aged men now. Those who knew their Des Moines of 10 or 20 years ago have never forgotten the genial Chinese face behind the counter. Dozens of fledging lawyers who ate with Lee that opening day are now addressed as 'Judge.' What night life Des Moines knew in the roistering days before the dry law was at Lee's." (Iowa's state lawmakers had approved a statewide prohibition in Iowa in 1916, four years before national Prohibition banned the production, importation, transportation and sale of alcoholic beverages in America from 1920 to 1933.)

"The after-theater crowd, the old college crowd, the newspaper bunch, the judges, the doctors and the actors will still throng Lee's, but Lee will be gone," the article added.

Appealing to a diverse crowd was part of the success for a place like King Ying Low. Lee told the *Tribune* that after he traveled to China to see his family, he'd return to Des Moines—probably. "You see, people here like me, and I like them," he said. "They treat me well. I treat them well. Maybe come back."

"But things won't be the same to the old crowd that knew Des Moines as a straggling country town with growing pains whose only touch of Bohemian life was Lee's place, until Lee returns," the *Tribune* concluded.

New Owners Took King Ying Low to New Levels

When King Ying Low announced its grand reopening in 1940 at its new location at 613 Grand Avenue, the restaurant promoted its Chinese food, fine steaks and chops from Casson's and Amend's meat purveyors. King Ying Low also served Swift's "delicious ice cream," along with milk and cream exclusively from the local Flynn Dairy. Meals were available from 6:00 a.m. to 2:00 a.m. If that weren't enough, the ad promised, "We deliver chop suey to your home."

By the 1970s, King Ying Low was known for a cuisine "short on American chop suey and long on the sophisticated Mandarin school of Chinese cookery, with Szechwan specialties there, also, as well as more familiar Cantonese," according to "A Chinese Adventure in D.M. Restaurant," which ran in the November 5, 1975 issue of the *Des Moines Tribune*.

Jean Tallman, the *Tribune's* food editor, noted that King Ying Low's four new cooks—including Ludwig Young (a fourth-generation Chinese American), Kwok-Foo Tse (head chef), Sung-Kit Tsui and Jack-Hung Yuen—came to the Midwest "'because that's where the adventure is' in Chinese cookery in this country."

Young had lived in San Francisco, New York and Philadelphia but knew that those cities had plenty of Chinese restaurants. When he found out that King Ying Low was available in Des Moines, he decided to seize this opportunity in October 1975. The quality of his food was good, Tallman noted.

The article added that sizzle is a distinction of Mandarin cuisine "and a piece of restauranting showmanship that's a delight to the diner." A sizzling dish is presented at the table in two serving dishes, the rice and the food to accompany it, which at King Ying Low was chicken in a fruit sauce; shrimp with mushrooms, bamboo shoots and greens; or a soup of abalone, sea cucumbers, Chinese cabbage, pork and mushrooms in chicken stock. If the rice wasn't hot enough, then it makes no noise and "therefore no sense," Ludwig explained.

Guests could enjoy sizzling rice soup with the Mandarin family dinner served for two or more people at $5.95 per person. Also on that dinner were fried shrimp, fried wontons, Mongolian beef, mu shu pork, Peking chow mein and steamed rice, with an "incredibly delicate" almond pudding, fortune cookies and Chinese green tea. "Perfection is the aim at King Ying Low," concluded the story.

Food critic Josef Mossman gave King Ying Low a notable four-star review in 1978, describing the experience as "dining sumptuously." Readers who commented on this through letters to the editor in the *Des Moines Tribune* described King Ying Low as one of Des Moines's most consistent fine restaurants. "All this and good service, too!" wrote a couple from Collins, Iowa.

"Resting On Its Laurels Instead of Its Mu Shu"

Times were changing, however, by the late 1980s. The October 26, 1989 edition of the *Des Moines Register* ran the article "Venerable King Ying Low Hasn't Kept Up with the Times: City's Original Chinese Restaurant Is Resting on Its Laurels Instead of Its Mu Shu." The article by J.R. Miller

After King Ying Low closed, its legacy lived on at Fong's Pizza, which opened on January 26, 2009, at 223 Fourth Street. Fong's crab rangoon pizza is a local favorite. *Author's collection.*

was blunt. "The egg drop soup that came with the luncheon specials was pretty bad," wrote Miller after dining at the restaurant at 223 Fourth Street. "The broth was nearly solidified with cornstarch, which really was the only flavor I could identify. Almond chicken was almond only if you count the few slivered ones sprinkled on top. The rest was chicken, celery and water chestnuts in a flavorless, cloudy sauce—certainly not inedible, but totally bland."

Also suffering from "blanditis" were the shrimp and peapods, "which were this and nothing more," according to Miller. "I would like to give unqualified praise to a place that has lasted more than eight decades, but I can't."

After King Ying Low closed around 2008, its legacy lived on. Fong's Pizza, located at Fourth Street in downtown Des Moines, opened on January 26, 2009. The Asian influence in Fong's menu and décor was inspired by King Ying Low, which had been located at Fong's site for years. Fong's caught the attention of Alton Brown, celebrity chef and Food Network star.

"You ready for this? Fong's Pizza is one of the coolest establishments I've ever been to. And I'm sad it's not closer to Atlanta," he said. "Let me set the scene for you: Chinese decor, tiki drinks and serious pizza. Eating there with my crew was the most fun we've had on the tour yet. I'd recommend the Crab Rangoon (it was incredible), we also ordered the Beef and Broccoli, as well as a couple slices of the special Jalapeño Mac and Cheese pizza. I can't wait to go back."

If you'd like to re-create a taste of King Ying Low from those days of the chop suey craze, here's a recipe to get you started. Since chop suey originated in leftovers, it's a great way to use up whatever's in the refrigerator. Chop suey means "mixed pieces" after all. Just don't overcook the vegetables—you want them to be crisp-tender. Also, don't be intimidated by the list of specialty ingredients. Items like Thai chili paste are available in the Asian sections of most well-stocked supermarkets, and they add a great flavor boost to all your Asian dishes.

Homemade Chop Suey

1 tablespoon canola oil
½ cup sliced scallions
2 cloves garlic, sliced
4 cups sliced cabbage (Napa is a good choice)
2 stalks celery, sliced
1 8-ounce can bamboo shoots, drained and thinly sliced
2 cups sliced shiitake mushrooms
¾ teaspoon sugar
1 cup chicken broth
1½ tablespoons soy sauce
1 tablespoon Thai chili paste
2 tablespoons toasted sesame oil
1½ tablespoons cornstarch, dissolved in 1 tablespoon mirin
2 cups cooked chicken, pork or beef
2 cups cooked white rice
chopped cilantro and sesame seeds for garnish (optional)
other vegetables such as bok choy, baby corn, water chestnuts or snow pea pods (optional)

In a large nonstick pan or wok, heat the canola oil over medium high heat. Add the scallions and garlic and sauté until softened. Add the cabbage, celery, bamboo shoots and mushrooms (and other vegetables, if you choose) and cook until the cabbage has wilted, about 3 to 4 minutes. Add the sugar, chicken broth, soy sauce, chili paste and sesame oil and cook for 3 additional minutes, or until the liquids have come to a boil. Add the cornstarch/mirin mixture (dry white wine or rice vinegar will also do instead of mirin, although you'll need to counteract the sourness with about a ½ teaspoon of sugar for every tablespoon you use) to thicken the sauce. Add the meat to heat through. Serve the chop suey on top of the rice with the chopped cilantro and sesame seeds to garnish. Serves 4.

DINING AT THE BOLTON & HAY CAFÉS

While a chop suey house like King Ying Low was all the rage in the early twentieth century, more common dining options throughout Des Moines were no-frills cafés. Among the most long lived of this era were the Bolton & Hay cafés.

Restaurants like this went hand in hand with the railroad. The first train to connect to Des Moines arrived on August 29, 1866, according to the Des Moines Public Library. Rail travel peaked between 1911 and 1917, with more than 10,500 miles of track across Iowa, noted the Iowa Department of Transportation.

In this era, eateries tended to be located close to railroad depots, where numerous passenger and freight trains stopped daily. This spurred the development of the Bolton & Hay restaurant chain (and later the Bolton & Hay foodservice supply company) in Des Moines. Lewis M. Bolton and Harry O. Hay founded Bolton & Hay in 1920. The two were first associated with the restaurant business in Springfield, Illinois, but came to Des Moines on October 2, 1920, to establish a restaurant in Iowa.

"My grandfather Lewis worked for the railroad early in his career," said Lew Bolton, president of Bolton & Hay and the third generation to carry on his family's business. "Just about every railroad station had a restaurant back then."

Bolton (who handled more of the inner workings of the business) and Hay (who was more of the sales/public relations guy) opened their first location in Des Moines on Saturday, November 13, 1920. Defying any superstitions, the restaurant contained thirteen barstools. On opening day, Bolton & Hay decided to serve free coffee and doughnuts from 9:00 a.m. to 5:00 p.m., after which food was served. The free coffee and doughnuts on opening day became a custom for every new Bolton & Hay restaurant, serving as an incentive for customers to stop by. The hope was that they would enjoy the experience so much that they'd return and become regular customers.

The restaurant business proved successful. In 1921, Harry Hay's brother-in-law, James Speicher Sr., came to Iowa from Pennsylvania to work for Bolton & Hay. The three men grew the business, which expanded to include eight Bolton & Hay restaurants in the Des Moines area.

Because Bolton & Hay restaurants offered twenty-four-hour service, there were never any locks on the doors, Bolton said. The only time the restaurants closed was to honor the national observance of respect during the burial of President Harding in 1923. At this time, the doors were simply tied shut, and the cashiers remained inside of the restaurants.

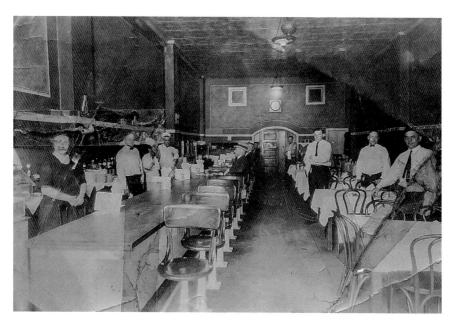

Bolton & Hay restaurants in Des Moines (like the one shown here in 1922) offered twenty-four-hour service. Bolton & Hay also runs a restaurant supply company that has served clients in Des Moines and beyond for a century. *Courtesy of Bolton & Hay.*

In addition to operating the restaurants, Bolton and Hay also started an equipment and restaurant supply company with a showroom, a cabinet shop, a sheet metal shop, a bakery and a butcher shop. This enabled the company to supply its own equipment and other supplies for its restaurants. Bolton and Hay also purchased three farms and produced all the milk needed for their restaurants from five herds of Holstein cows. One of the farms was located north of Bondurant, Bolton noted.

Bolton & Hay restaurants' focus was simple: serve good food at moderate prices with quick, courteous service. Slogans for the restaurants included "Hungry? Come In" and "They Have No Equal." The one that stuck was "'Tis the Taste that Tells the Tale."

During the Great Depression, Bolton & Hay's business shrank by nearly 40 percent in 1932–33. Bolton & Hay reduced prices at its restaurants by about 20 percent, featuring a twenty-five-cent noon meal and five-cent egg sandwiches. The business made it through this difficult time and eventually rebounded, said Bolton, who keeps archives of the company's handwritten records from those days.

By 1939, Bolton & Hay had served 38,650 pounds of sausage, 304,494 pounds of beef, 89,242 pounds of pork, 78,195 gallons of milk, 24,000 bottles of catsup, 78,544 pies and 40,434 pounds of coffee.

After Harry Hay died in 1947 and Lewis Bolton retired in 1948, the second generation of their families took over the business. By the early 1960s, the company's leaders were using an airplane to make sales calls throughout Iowa and the Midwest.

Business continued to thrive at the Bolton & Hay cafés. By the early 1960s, menus included cream of chicken soup for twenty-five cents, Jell-O for twenty cents, hamburgers for forty cents, baked ham for fifty-five cents, choice Iowa beef tips in mushroom sauce for one dollar and strawberry shortcake for forty cents. Diners could wash it all down with a variety of beverages, including coffee, Pepsi and Teem pop (Teem was a lemon/lime-flavored soft drink produced by the Pepsi-Cola Company starting in the 1960s), all for fifteen cents each.

Times were changing, however. As growth in the Des Moines metro area continued to push into the suburbs, all of the Bolton & Hay restaurants were sold by the late 1960s. By then, Bolton & Hay had served more than 50 million customers.

After the restaurants closed, Bolton & Hay focused exclusively on the foodservice supply and equipment part of the business. After constructing a new thirty-thousand-square-foot building at 2701 Delaware Avenue, Bolton

By the time all the Bolton & Hay restaurants had been sold by the late 1960s, the company had served more than 50 million customers. *Courtesy of Bolton & Hay.*

& Hay featured a modern showroom, a warehouse, offices, a cabinet shop, a sheet metal shop and a butcher shop. Craftsmen at the cabinet shop, which operated from the 1940s to the mid-1980s, built everything from pie cases to counters to cigarette cases, said Bolton, who worked part time at the company, including the cabinet shop, throughout high school and college. "It was a sense of accomplishment when you set up a new installation and saw the restaurant go into business."

Through the years, longtime Bolton & Hay customers from Des Moines have included the Younkers Tea Room, Tursi's Latin King, the Wakonda Club, local schools and other organizations. The ability to adapt to changing times and keep up with new products and technology is the key to staying in business for a century, said Bolton, who joined the company full time in 1982.

"In our one-hundred-year history we've done business with half the states in America, and we've shipped products overseas to places like Saudi Arabia," said Bolton, who works with his team of eight employees at 4333 Park Avenue, where the company moved in December 2018. "We're proud to be a locally owned, family-operated business that's still based in Des Moines."

❖ ❖ ❖

Bolton & Hay Butter Cookies

Homestyle cooking defined Bolton & Hay restaurants across Des Moines for nearly fifty years. This classic Bolton & Hay recipe is so vintage it refers to placing the cookie dough in an ice box rather than a refrigerator. Why chill the dough? Room-temperature butter is more likely to stick to your work surface than cold butter and, consequently, requires extra flour when rolling out the dough. This leads to less tender cookies.

1 cup butter
1 cup granulated sugar
2 eggs
1 teaspoon white vinegar
1 teaspoon vanilla (or almond extract)
3 cups all-purpose flour
2 teaspoons baking powder
¼ teaspoon salt

Cream butter. Add sugar and cream the mixture thoroughly. Add eggs into mixture and beat thoroughly. Add vinegar and vanilla to mixture.

In a separate bowl, sift flour with baking powder and salt. Combine flour mixture with butter mixture. Shape dough into a roll. Wrap dough in waxed paper. Place in ice box (or refrigerator) for at least 1 hour before rolling the dough.

Roll dough on a floured surface. (Modern tip: Rolling the dough between sheets of nonstick parchment or waxed paper will make the process even easier. Roll dough to ¼-inch or ⅛-inch thickness, depending on your preference.) Cut cookies to desired shape and place on ungreased baking sheet. Bake at 375 degrees Fahrenheit for approximately 5 to 7 minutes, or until cookie edges are lightly browned. Cool completely.

Note: If you'd rather make chocolate cookies, the Bolton & Hay recipe notes that you should use 1½ cups of sugar (instead of just 1 cup), along with 2 squares of chocolate.

CHAPTER 2

Authentic Italian Influences

A s Des Moines grew and its dining options evolved, Italian food put the city's restaurants on the map in the twentieth century. "It has been widely—sometimes snidely—remarked that eating out in Des Moines seems to be all steak and Italian," noted the *Datebook* section of the *Des Moines Tribune* on January 18, 1979, which ran Pat Denato's story "A Big Ciao for Italian Chow." "So? Is there something wrong with having a plentitude of good cooks whose creations say 'Viva Italia?'"

Eating the Italian way in Des Moines has always been a feast for the senses. Even as Italian American immigrants in Des Moines adapted ingredients that were available in Iowa, their cooking always paid homage to their homeland. Nowhere was this more evident than the south side of Des Moines, which became known as "Little Italy." From the early 1880s through the 1930s, several thousand Italian immigrants, mainly from the southern provinces of Italy, relocated to Des Moines to find a more prosperous way of life, noted Jacqueline Comito in her 1995 Iowa State University thesis "*Porco Sei*; *Porti Are*: The Autobiography of an Italian American family in Des Moines."

The vast majority (75 percent) of Des Moines's Italian Americans originated from the Calabrese culture, Comito noted. Calabria is located at the rugged toe of the boot in Southern Italy. While the region includes beautiful landscapes and agricultural areas, Southern Italy and Sicily were plagued by grinding rural poverty a century ago.

Between around 1880 and 1924, more than 4 million Italians immigrated to the United States, half of them between 1900 and 1910 alone—with the

As Des Moines grew and its dining options evolved, Italian food put the city's restaurants on the map. The Italian American Heritage Center on Des Moines's south side showcases this history. *Author's collection.*

majority coming from Southern Italy, according to PBS.org's Destination America. "Entire villages emptied out in the exodus to America and other places that offered a better life or, at the least, a full stomach," noted the National Geographic book *Tasting Italy: A Culinary Journey* in its description of Calabria.

Many of the Italian immigrants who settled in Iowa a century ago found work in two booming industries: coal mining and the railroad. Mining was a physically demanding, dirty job that coated the workers' skin with grime. When these men emerged from the mine after a long work day, they were as black as guinea fowl. While Italian grinder sandwiches were once called "guinea grinders" at Des Moines restaurants and the Iowa State Fair, this slur was dropped by the 1990s.

This recipe for Italian grinders comes from Chef George Formaro, a Des Moines native who grew up on sausage and other fine products from Graziano Bros. Italian Foods. This grocery/deli has served Des Moines since 1912, when the business was founded by Calabrese immigrants Frank and Louie Graziano.

Italian Grinders

*2 pounds fennel Italian sausage (Graziano's sausage is worth the road trip
to Des Moines)
1 15-ounce can tomato sauce
½ teaspoon garlic powder
½ teaspoon onion powder
1 pinch dry basil
hoagie buns
mozzarella cheese*

Cook sausage, stirring constantly. When sausage is done, add all remaining ingredients, except the buns and cheese. Cook on low heat for another 20 to 30 minutes, stirring constantly. Place sausage mixture into hoagie buns and top with mozzarella cheese. Place the Italian grinders in a preheated, 400-degree oven or a toaster oven until bread is toasted and cheese is melted.

ANJO'S REFLECTED COAL MINING HERITAGE

At the height of the coal mining boom in Iowa, from 1895 to 1925, hundreds of mines operated in Iowa, not just in Des Moines but in counties like Polk, Dallas, Boone, Webster and Appanoose. During this era, Iowa's mining industry employed as many as eighteen thousand people, and the industry ranked second only to agriculture in Iowa's economy, noted Iowa State University historian Dorothy Schwieder in her book *Black Diamonds: Life and Work in Iowa's Coal Mining Communities*.

Italian immigrant families who worked in the mines and on the railroads helped Des Moines and central Iowa grow. By 1920, Des Moines's population had reached 126,468, a nearly 127 percent jump from 1890. While the growth of the city slowed in the next few decades, it was steady, reaching 208,982 residents by 1960.

Some of the restaurateurs who brought the flavors of Italy to the Des Moines area got their start in towns around the capital city. The Boone County town of Madrid was home to Angelina "Ann" Tancredi, who grew up in the coal mining culture of the Madrid area. Her skills in gardening and Italian cooking took root in this area.

Tancredi and her husband, Harry (who grew up in Florence, Italy), started their popular restaurant Anjo's in Madrid in 1948 before moving it to the Des Moines area (6587 University Avenue in Windsor Heights). Although it closed permanently in 1991, Anjo's is still remembered for its unforgettable, authentic Italian cuisine.

Anjo's Italian restaurant was still in Madrid when Jean Tallman, food editor, detailed its "sophisticated Florentine cooking" in the November 12, 1956 issue of the *Des Moines Tribune*. The old adage "the customer is always right" didn't apply here. "There are lots of things wrong with his customers, he feels," wrote Tallman, describing Harry Tancredi. "And he insists on doing them and their stomachs a service by making them eat as he says, not as they want to. This man who dares boss the customers is Harry Tancredi, owner of Anjo's Italian restaurant here and one of the most colorful characters in the food business in Iowa."

If you wanted to sip a glass of ice water as you waited for your order at Anjo's back then, it wouldn't happen with Harry Tancredi, even if you said "please." "I won't allow you to waste your money and my time by drinking anything cold while waiting for my food," he told Tallman for the article "No Ice Water at His Place: Madrid Restaurateur Dares to 'Boss' Customers."

Ice water is an astringent that deadens the taste buds and contracts the stomach, Harry Tancredi said. Diners who dared asked for coffee with their meal received a "dissertation on the glories of the brew, then a reprimand for even intimating that coffee is compatible with dinner."

"If you insist on coffee with spumoni (the wonderful Italian ice cream rich with almonds, candied orange peel and maraschino cherries), or with biscotti tortoni (frozen custard crunchy with crumbled macaroons), you will get it," Tallman wrote. "But Harry prefers coffee as a final course, maybe just coffee, but, preferably, double-strength demitasse."

Request a bottle of ketchup or steak sauce and you're confronted with a blank stare. "He tolerates neither and doesn't even have them in the kitchen," Tallman wrote. "Harry says his wife, Ann, cooks food to be eaten, not to be tampered with."

The most vocal disapproval, however, often came with pizza orders. Customers who liked mushrooms, onions or green peppers on their pizza could go elsewhere for such a concoction. "And you'll be invited to in rather strong words," Tallman said. "Italian pizza is only cheese and tomato, and Harry will accept no tomfoolery."

His only concession to an Iowan's version of Italian pizza was sausage pizza. But any old sausage wouldn't do. Harry Tancredi made his own sausage with basil, marjoram, thyme and Italian parsley from his family's garden.

What manner of man was this who dared defy the customer? Harry Tancredi was a former banker who liked food more than money, Tallman said. Born in Northern Italy, he immigrated to Philadelphia, Pennsylvania, when he was young. He attended the Wharton School of Finance at the University of Pennsylvania and became the manager of the foreign department of a Wilkes-Barre, Pennsylvania bank. "Banking wasn't any fun, according to Harry's thinking. But cooking was," Tallman wrote.

Harry Tancredi bought an Italian restaurant in Pennsylvania and later managed restaurants in Las Vegas and Los Angeles before coming to Madrid, his wife's hometown. There was no Italian décor in the Tancredi's Italian restaurant. With its chrome and plastic, booths and stools, it looked like any other small-town Iowa café, "except that it shines more than most," Tallman said. "Inspiration for a dish comes from Harry, who tests and tastes, adds this and that until it suits. Ann, a charming woman who looks like a well-scrubbed madonna, is the cook."

Harry Tancredi didn't think highly of American food. "Food here is much too fried," he explained. "And in restaurants, there's no variety. Same food week after week. A shame when such fine food is raised right at the back door," he added. (Sounds like Tancredi was well ahead of his time and would have embraced the farm-to-table culinary philosophy that began transforming Iowa restaurant food in the 2000s.) He did admit, however, that Iowa steaks were superb.

"If you feel that fine food is worth waiting for, Anjo's is for you," Tallman added. "It is no place for a customer in a hurry, because foods are prepared after they are ordered. You'll find no steam table here."

Tancredi's Pollo al Marsala (Anjo's Chicken in Wine Sauce)

When Jean Tallman, food editor for the *Des Moines Tribune*, asked Harry Tancredi in 1956 to jot down a recipe for one of his specialties, it started out like this: "Tagliate a pezzi un pollo da tre libbre e fategli prendere colore in padella con burro e cipolla—" With the help of his wife, Ann Tancredi, Tallman offered this translation for Pollo al Marsala.

Disjoint a 3-pound frying chicken and brown in butter. Add 1 teaspoon chopped onion and 1 cup dry white wine. Bring to a boil and boil hard until wine is evaporated and absorbed into meat.

Sprinkle 2 tablespoons of flour in pan and add 2 cups chicken broth. Season with salt and pepper. Simmer until broth is reduced by half. Squeeze in juice from half a lemon and add 1 teaspoon chopped parsley.

Arrange chicken pieces in center of platter and top with pan drippings, which have thickened to sauce consistency because of the flour. Garnish platter with a Roman specialty, tiny green peas cooked with prosciutto and onion.

Manicotti (Cheese-Filled Noodles in Tomato Sauce)

This recipe from Anjo's also appeared in the 1956 *Des Moines Tribune* article featuring the restaurant.

2 cups flour
1 tablespoon butter
3 eggs
½ teaspoon salt
1 cup lukewarm water
basil
parsley
1 pound of ricotta or soft-curd cottage cheese
2 cups tomato sauce or spaghetti sauce
½ cup freshly grated Parmesan cheese

Combine flour, butter, eggs and salt. Add water a little at a time to form a rather soft dough. Knead until smooth. Roll dough on board to a ⅛-inch thickness. Cut into 4-by-6-inch rectangles.

Add some basil and parsley (fresh, if possible) to ricotta cheese or cottage cheese to suit your taste. Place 1½ tablespoons of the cheese mixture in center of each rectangle of dough. Roll dough and close by pressing edges firmly.

Boil manicotti gently about 10 minutes in a large pan of salted water. Remove manicotti carefully, one by one, with flat strainer or perforated spatula and place in large, flat casserole dish. Cover manicotti with tomato or spaghetti sauce, sprinkle with more basil and bake at 400 degrees for about 10 minutes. Serve with grated Parmesan cheese. Makes 6 servings.

ALICE'S SPAGHETTILAND THRIVED IN WAUKEE

Like Anjo's, some of the Des Moines area's beloved Italian restaurants weren't actually in Des Moines. That was the case with Alice's Spaghettiland in Waukee, west of Des Moines. Like Anjo's, Alice's Spaghettiland proved that coal mining communities could empower women to become successful entrepreneurs.

Coal mining had become big business in the Waukee area by 1920. The Shuler Coal Mine, which operated from 1921 to 1949, provided jobs in the winter for many immigrants from Italy and central Europe. Starting in 1947, Waukee was home to Alice's Spaghettiland, run by Alice Nizzi, the daughter of an Italian immigrant, in the Shuler mining community just north of Hickman Road.

This family-style restaurant, which was located in a house, certainly wasn't pretentious. It was the kind of place where Nizzi took an interest in her customers and got to know them. It was operated exclusively by women, including Alice and her sister, Anita. Waitresses were required to wear white,

Starting in 1947, Waukee was home to Alice's Spaghettiland, run by Alice Nizzi in the Shuler mining community. Alice's closed in 2004. *Courtesy of Waukee Area Historical Society.*

starched uniforms. People would come from around the area, including Des Moines, to enjoy a meal at Alice's Spaghettiland. "Alice was famous not just for pasta, but for her fried chicken," said Connie Wimer, owner and chairman of Business Publications in Des Moines. "We'd take our own wine there to enjoy with our meal."

After Alice's closed in 2004, the Waukee Area Historical Society began hosting fundraising dinners in the spring featuring Alice's spaghetti and Italian salad. Hundreds of people attend this popular event.

Alice's legacy also lives on in the virtual world, thanks to the "I Love Alice's Spaghettiland" Facebook group. "I always looked forward to going there," wrote Leslie Horning-Carlson. "Alice always came out to greet us. Wow, such delicious food! I used to put my French fries in my spaghetti, then nobody would try to eat my leftovers! I would give anything to do that again."

BAMIE KEPT DES MOINES WELL FED—AND LAUGHING

While Alice's was legendary for spaghetti, many of Des Moines's Italian restaurants made a name for themselves with their pizza, with some serving up this wonderful new creation (at least it was new to most Iowans) as early as the late 1940s. "There was an Italian American restaurant explosion in Des Moines by the early 1950s, with pizza becoming the big thing after 1952," said Chef George Formaro, a Des Moines native, esteemed restaurateur and food historian.

By the late 1950s and early 1960s, pizza had its own section in the yellow pages of the Des Moines phone book. "I'd argue that Des Moines is one of the best pizza towns around," added Formaro, who noted that every Des Moines neighborhood has had its own pizza joint. Downtown had Babe's. The north side had Chuck's. And the south side had Bamie's Pizza House. Oh boy, who could forget Bamie's?

"Picture yourself sitting at a restaurant, peacefully enjoying dinner, when a loud siren starts to wail," wrote Richard Somerville in a piece called "Son of Grumpy Gourmet," which ran in the October 22, 1980 edition of the *Des Moines Tribune*. "People look up at the ceiling, under their table—what's going on? Through the door bursts a fireman in bunker gear, including a helmet, carrying a carbon dioxide fire extinguisher."

"Where's the fire?" he shouts. As one group shrugs, he points the extinguisher under their table and fires it off with a *whoosh*, sending ladies screaming and men jumping. No one is safe as the fireman scurries around like Groucho Marx. A pool player gets a chilling blast and sends the cue ball flying.

"As the phantom madman disappears behind the bar, are people enraged, threatening to call their lawyers? No, they are here to enjoy the show. At Bamie's, the show is Frank 'Bamie' Bonanno, madcap extraordinaire," Somerville said.

Bamie was also a dream come true for writers. "The unmarked green building on the south side of town looks like some joint that sells mufflers or shocks that have no warranty," noted an article called "Datebook's Crustworthy Test," which appeared in the *Des Moines Tribune* on February 16, 1981. "You get plenty of shocks all right—along with what our Datebook taste-testers consider the best pizza in town."

"Inside, owner Frank 'Bamie' Bonanno is tugging at a ratty women's hairpiece (which some recalled looking like matted hair from a sink trap) on his head as a crowd of pizza lovers looks on," the article continued. "'Is my wig on straight? Is my tie alright?' he asked with mock concern, shooing off one young man with a giant fly swatter and zapping another with a jet of water from a fire extinguisher."

If you didn't know Bamie, you might think the guy was a jerk. But those who knew him loved him. "He'd give anybody a helping hand," said Frank Graziano, a co-owner of Graziano Bros. grocery who was quoted in a *Des Moines Register* interview. "He was a wonderful person."

Invariably, longtime customers couldn't resist bringing a rookie along with them to Bamie's back in the day. It was especially fun to observe customers experiencing Bamie's for their first (and occasionally) last time. "Hey Bamie, my friend needs water," they'd shout. "You say you need water?" Bamie asked. The rookie would get a shot of water in the face, recalled one *Des Moines Register* reporter. Just to make sure there were no hard feelings, Bamie offered to take the soaked person's picture. The "camera" shot water too.

It was show time all the time at Bamie's Pizza House, located at 1920 Army Post Road at the intersection of Fleur Drive. This is where red lights flashed, sirens screamed and Bamie's trombone (with a boxing glove attached at the end) blatted awful noises, all while making a dangerous swoop over the heads of screaming friends. On any given night, there was a good chance that the jukebox was also blaring tunes like Frank Sinatra's rendition of "Bad, Bad, Leroy Brown," one of Bamie's all-time favorites.

Bamie's routinely won awards for the best pizza in Des Moines, based on *Datebook* taste tests and other criteria. When the *Des Moines Tribune* announced its "Polk County Pizza Champs" in September 1970, Bamie's made the top

Above: Frank "Bamie" Bonanno, owner of Bamie's Pizza House, loved pranks, like pointing his fire extinguisher under guests' tables and firing it off with a *whoosh. Courtesy of Ron Bonanno.*

Right: Bamie's Pizza House, a south side favorite, routinely won awards for the best pizza in Des Moines. On their busiest nights, the Bonanno family would cook 150 to 200 pizzas. *Author's collection.*

five, along with Des Moines legends like Babe's restaurant downtown. The accolades never stopped after that.

Neither did the pranks. People loved to watch Bamie fling mugs of beer down the bar or hold his fake mouse in front of somebody's nose. "That guy was just so alive," said George Formaro, who recalled eating at Bamie's when he was growing up. "You couldn't create that kind of wackiness. It was authentic."

Homemade with "Lots of Love"

Bamie was born on April 22, 1926, in Des Moines to Italian immigrant parents Frank and Grace Bonanno. "Our family came from Southern Italy, from Calabria and Sicily," noted Bamie's son Ron Bonanno, who lives in West Des Moines.

Bamie was raised on Jackson Street on the south side of Des Moines, not far from the Graziano Bros. grocery store. "Bamie" was a nickname inherited during his football-playing days at Dowling Catholic High School.

"My uncle Armand was going to go to the University of Alabama to play football in 1938," Bonanno said. "They called him Big Bama, which got shortened to Big Bam. My dad was also a talented football player, and people started calling him Little Bama, which became Bamie."

Bamie lettered in football, baseball and basketball during his high school career. After graduating from Dowling in 1944, Bamie started working as a bartender around Des Moines in 1948. His older brother Armand ran a place called Armand's Lounge at the corner of Merle Hay Road and Meredith Drive—the western edge of Des Moines back then. This is where Bamie learned how to make pizza in the mid-1950s.

In the late 1950s, you could get a small pizza at Armand's Lounge for $0.75, while a large pizza was $1.25. Toppings included anchovies, sausage, pepperoni, ham and mushrooms. If you were willing to drop some extra cash, you could get shrimp pizza (a small for $1.00 or a large for $1.50). "When Dad started making pizza dough, it was so bad you could throw it at the wall and the dough would shatter," Bonanno said.

Fortunately, Bamie's older sister, Sadie, schooled him in the fine points of dough making. Homemade dough, homemade pizza sauce and homemade sausage became the trademarks of Bamie's pizza when he opened his own place in 1963. His wife, Colleen, worked right beside him at Bamie's Pizza House. "She was the hardest working soul in that restaurant," said Bonanno, whose father and mother had met at a dance at the Val-Air Ballroom in West Des Moines. "Mom could roll pizzas like no one else."

All five of the Bonanno kids grew up working in the restaurant, which opened for business five days a week (Monday, Wednesday, Thursday, Friday and Saturday) at 5:00 p.m. Bamie would often stay until 3:00 a.m., long after the last customer had gone home, to get all the work done. Sometimes he had a little extra help in the evening. "If parents had kids who were prone to getting in trouble, they'd say, 'Bamie, put 'em to work,'" Bonanno recalled. "Dad would have them clean tables and handle other jobs around the restaurant."

Other than that, Bamie's relied mainly on family labor. "As a kid, I washed dishes that were bigger than me, like the vat we cooked the stromboli in," said Bonanno, who started working at Bamie's at age ten. "I also mixed pizza dough thirty pounds at a time."

On their busiest nights, the Bonanno family would cook 150 to 200 pizzas. Some of the most requested toppings at Bamie's included sausage and green pepper or sausage and mushroom. "Mom's favorite was cheese and onion," Bonanno said. "Her theory was that a basic cheese pizza shows the quality of the pizza."

Food critics praised all facets of Bamie's pizzas. "The thin crust is outstanding, and the pizza sauce has a delicious sweet tinge that sets it apart," wrote Richard Somerville in a piece called "Son of Grumpy Gourmet," which ran in the October 22, 1980 edition of the *Des Moines Tribune*.

Other food reviewers praised the sausage and the quality of the cheese. When people tried to coax the pizza recipe from Bamie, he said it was his own recipe developed from lots of hard work. When asked if he used any secret ingredients, he said, "Lots of love."

Serving Up the Zaniest Antics in Town

Bamie didn't run ads in the yellow pages of the phone book, and he didn't have a sign out front, according to the *Datebook* article. "If they don't know where we're at, they don't need to come," was Bamie's philosophy.

The only notice that you received about Bamie's was a small strip on the glass door that cautioned, "Enter at your own risk." Bamie said some attorney told him put that up there—just in case.

There was no menu at Bamie's, Somerville noted in his food review. Customers would walk up to the bar and tell the Bonannos what toppings they wanted. Somerville's group had a large (nine-inch) sausage, pepperoni and mushroom pizza for $4.50 and a small (seven-inch) ham pizza for $3.50.

"As a bonus, Bamie's offers ham and cheese and stromboli (sausage) sandwiches," Somerville noted. "My wife, the sausage sandwich expert, tried one of the $2 strombolis—a huge section of Italian bread stuffed with spicy sausage and mozzarella cheese—and pronounced it the best in town, bar none."

But you still needed a thick skin—and possibly a raincoat—to dine at Bamie's, Somerville concluded. "As we left, Bamie said, 'No hard feelings,' and invited us to the bar to give us lollipops. 'Here, take a bunch,' he cooed, 'and here's a water chaser!' He lifted a water fire-extinguisher onto the counter as we ran for the front door. We didn't make it."

Bamie admitted that he could sometimes go overboard. "I don't try to be mean," he told a reporter once. "I try to have fun, but sometimes fun can get carried away. I've always been silly."

People appreciated Bamie's sense of humor and often contributed to his collection of hats, which he would wear around the restaurant. Vintage pictures show him sporting everything from a cowboy hat to a nautical captain's hat.

"We went to Bamie's frequently in the late 1960s when we lived in Des Moines during the first six years of our marriage," said Carol Jo Wold, who grew up on a farm near Lytton, Iowa. "My husband, Ben, worked at Ford Implement on Southeast Thirteenth Street, and I taught school in Indianola. We loved going to Bamie's with our next-door neighbors, who were our good friends. We were all young couples in our twenties before we had kids. The atmosphere at Bamie's was great, with the noise, energy and 'Bad, Bad Leroy Brown' on the jukebox. Bamie's owner Frank Bonanno served good pizza that filled you up with just a slice or two."

With its location near the Des Moines Airport, Bamie's attracted an interesting clientele, including Henry Mancini, who wrote the famous theme to the *Peter Gunn* television series, as well as the music for *The Pink Panther* film series. "Henry Mancini came in one time and declared Bamie's had some of the best pizza he'd ever eaten in the world," Bonanno said.

Bamie's local patrons included *Des Moines Register* feature writer John Karras and columnist Donald Kaul, who created the Register's Annual Great Bicycle Ride Across Iowa (RAGBRAI) in 1973, which became the longest, largest and oldest recreational bicycle touring event in the world.

Back when Iowa PBS's (formerly Iowa Public Television) studios were located on the south side of Des Moines on Bell Avenue, employees would often stop by Bamie's for food and drinks. They even made a sixteen-minute documentary about Bamie's Pizza House in 1983, which can be viewed online at the YouTube social media platform. The public television team also presented Bamie with a large, colorful caricature of him, with the words "Thanks for Being Frank" surrounded by their signatures.

Changes at the Des Moines Airport led to the demise of Bamie's restaurant just a few years later. "Bamie is being forced to get out, in effect, in order to give airplanes a place to crash," noted the story "Bamie's Party Marks End of Restauranteur's Pizza Parlor Madness," which ran in the June 25, 1986 edition of the *Des Moines Register*.

Frank "Bamie" Bonanno (*left*) worked alongside his family, including his son Ron, who started working at Bamie's Pizza House at age ten. Ron mixed pizza dough thirty pounds at a time. *Courtesy of Ron Bonanno.*

What a party it was at that plain green restaurant that stood in an area the Federal Aviation Administration declared a "clear zone," to be vacated in case planes ever crash there. "The last night Bamie's was open, Dad gave everything away, including twenty-three kegs of beer," Bonanno recalled.

The *Register* article asked, "Has Frank Bonanno hammered his last chicken? Bonanno, the most beloved and certifiably wacko businessman in Des Moines, will soon have no place to pound poultry, squirt water on customers, or even blast them with freezing fire extinguishers."

The chicken referred to one of Bamie's famous lines. After bellowing, "Who ordered chicken salad?" Bamie would yank a rubber chicken from under the bar and pound it with whatever was handy. Bamie could make even the orneriest customer laugh, recalled Jim Willson, an insurance salesman and longtime customer quoted in the article.

As Bamie, now sixty, pondered the demolition of his restaurant, he was frustrated. "I've worked hard to build something for my family, and now the city wants to take it away from me," he told the *Register*. "I'm too old to start from scratch. I put my blood into this and paid for it with two heart attacks and open-heart surgery. I don't think I could do it again."

A simple note, written by hand in pencil, captured this raw emotion as it notified loyal customers about the closure of the restaurant. "Bamie's Pizza House, our pride and joy, will be gone after Aug. 2, 1986. The day that broke our hearts."

While Ron Bonanno's original goal was to carry on Bamie's tradition and open the restaurant again by 1989, things didn't work out that way. His mother was fine with that, he added. "When you see your dad work so many hours and have three heart attacks, including his first one at age forty-two, it changes your outlook."

Bonanno, who enjoyed a thirty-year career with Des Moines–based Joseph's Jewelers, credited his success with the lessons his parents taught him at Bamie's, including the importance of hard work and a willingness to serve people.

Nearly seven years after Bamie's closed, Bamie passed away at age sixty-seven in May 1993 after suffering a heart attack during Mass at Christ the King Catholic Church in Des Moines. The *Des Moines Register* honored him with the feature story "Bamie: He Left Des Moines Laughing."

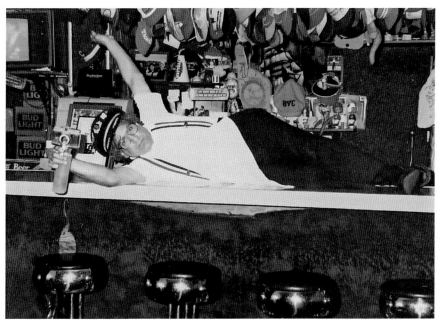

It was show time all the time at Bamie's Pizza House, thanks to Frank "Bamie" Bonanno, dubbed a "madcap extraordinaire" by the local press. Bamie's closed in 1986. *Courtesy of Ron Bonanno.*

"Let's assume that St. Peter, having seen his fair share of characters through the ages, is not easily surprised," wrote Ken Fuson. "Wait until he gets a load of Bamie. He'll be the wig-wearing, chicken-pounding, water-spraying pizza maker from Des Moines. 'Hiya, shorty,' you can hear him say. 'You say you need water?'"

To call Bamie a colorful character was an understatement, Fuson added. "The bicentennial fireworks were colorful. Bamie was a one-man amusement park, a perpetual-motion machine, the missing Marx brother."

In a lot of ways, Bamie was like famed Des Moines restaurateur Babe Bisignano, added Van Harden, host of WHO Newsradio 1040's *Van Harden in the Morning* show. "Some people went to their restaurants for the food, and others went to experience these guys and their larger-than-life personalities."

Bamie himself remains a Des Moines restaurant icon. "I'm so proud of that," Bonanno said. "Dad made a lot of people happy."

DES MOINES ABOUNDED WITH ITALIAN AMERICAN SPECIALTIES

The spirit of hospitality that defined Bamie's Pizza House was also evident in many other Italian restaurants that have flourished in Des Moines through the years. Gary Fatino's, a south side favorite on Fleur Drive in the 1970s, served dinner specialties including saltimbocca; chicken, veal or eggplant parmigiana; Italian-style chicken livers; fettucine Alfredo and osso buco (braised veal shanks in tomato sauce with carrots and onions)—all in an elegant setting complete with chandeliers.

For the better part of four decades, Helen & Pat's was famous for cavatelli, a favorite menu item named for the small curled pasta used in the dish. The restaurant's flagship sprung up on the north side before sprouting franchised establishments across the metro. Helen & Pat's eventually faded away at the dawn of the twenty-first century, noted the *Des Moines Register*'s 2019 story "Gone but Not Forgotten: 41 Popular Des Moines Restaurants Now Closed."

Sam & Gabe's, which Jerry Talerico opened in the late 1990s, served Italian specialties, from stuffed cannelloni to lemon mousse cheesecake. Sam & Gabe's had two locations (Des Moines's East Village and Urbandale) by the time it closed in 2018.

Also in 2019, Mama Lacona's Italian Restaurant, located at 3825 121st Street in Urbandale, closed permanently on August 31 after serving homemade dishes to hungry customers for more than six decades.

"Through the years, Mama Lacona's has served classic Italian recipes passed down from the late Teresa Lacona—formerly Teresa Tursi—who many consider the great-grandmother of Italian cuisine in Des Moines," noted the *Des Moines Register*.

Family has been the key to so many of Des Moines's Italian American restaurants, past and present. It's a legacy worth savoring.

CHAPTER 3

Babe, You've Got What It Takes

When you talk about classic restaurants of Des Moines, there's one name that people of a certain age always mention, even if they never lived in Des Moines. It's Babe, as in Alphonse "Babe" Bisignano.

"I think, not to be boasting, there isn't a town of a hundred population that I can't go down the street and somebody will know who I am," Babe told *Des Moines* magazine when he was featured in the cover story "Babe Bisignano: Millionaire Bus Boy" in the April 1986 edition.

When Babe's biographer, Chuck Offenburger, called Babe "the best-known character in Iowa and beyond," that was no exaggeration. Babe was "an elegant character, often outrageous, the likes of which will not be seen again in our time."

There was a time when more people probably had their first drink, first date, wedding party or anniversary party at Babe's Italian restaurant on Sixth Avenue in downtown Des Moines than any other place in Iowa.

"Presidential candidates go there, stars of music and movies and media go there, and so do top coaches and athletes," Offenburger wrote in 1989. "And they mingle and revel in that plush atmosphere of food, drink, tradition and a hint of naughtiness that's all wound up in the place's bootlegging past. The old bootlegger himself—or call him the millionaire bus boy if you prefer—is never far away with a free drink and an outrageous story."

LEARNING FROM THE SCHOOL OF HARD KNOCKS

Babe came from the old school, a child of Italian immigrants who did well and never forgot how hard it was to do it.

Alphonse James Bisignano was born on March 14, 1913, in Des Moines to Genaro ("George") and Lena Bisignano. Genaro had immigrated to the United States from Terravecchia, Italy, while Lena was a native of Naples, Italy.

The Bisignanos lived in "Little Italy" on Des Moines's south side, first on Granger Avenue and then on Courtland Avenue. Lena would fix meals for people who came to the Bisignano home (mainly Irish and Jewish people from around the area). It was never a real restaurant, but she did a good business. She also made homebrewed beer and wine.

Babe remembered when his mother got raided by the cops when he was about nine years old. One day, when he came home from school, the county sheriff was opening his mother's kegs and pouring the alcohol down the drain in those Prohibition days.

Lena, the rock of the family, died at age thirty-five in 1923 during an operation. Genaro abandoned the family within five years of Lena's death. He told his kids that he was leaving for Chicago to find work and would send money. He never even sent a postcard. "No point in being bitter about it now," Babe told Offenburger years later. "Yeah, it was real hard, but if I hadn't had that kind of childhood, I wouldn't have made it as far as I have."

Babe started working part time when he was just a boy. As a ten-year-old, he'd be up by 5:00 a.m., standing at the corner of Sixth Avenue and Mulberry Street in Des Moines selling newspapers. He'd protect his turf from bullies who wanted to butt in on his business of buying the papers for a penny and selling them for two cents on the busiest corner he could find and defend. He'd repeat the operation later in the day when the evening papers came out. By the time he was an adolescent, Babe had found work shining shoes at local barbershops. "My mind was always on making a buck," Babe said.

After Genaro skipped town, Babe's school years were officially over. He entered the School of Hard Knocks, landing a job as a "go-fer" at the Des Moines Golf and Country Club, where he lived in the locker room. He'd caddy for the golfers, run errands for the men playing poker and procure the alcohol the men used to spike their "near beer."

After working at a meatpacking company and a car-body sander in the old Ford plant in Des Moines, Babe started boxing at "smokers," where businessmen at conventions would hire young guys to box for the entertainment. In 1929, Babe went to see Pinkie George at the boxing

Alphonso "Babe" Bisignano

Perhaps no Des Moines restaurateur was more famous than Alphonse "Babe" Bisignano. Babe, a professional boxer and wrestler as a young man, was a child of Italian immigrants who did well and never forgot how hard it was to do it. *Courtesy of Italian American Heritage Center.*

promotion office at the Des Moines Coliseum (which was destroyed by a fire in 1949 and preceded Veterans Memorial Auditorium). That's when sixteen-year-old Alphonse Bisignano became "Baby Carnera," inspired by Primo Carnera, an Italian professional boxer and wrestler, and started on the path to a better life.

At five feet, eleven inches and 175 pounds, Baby Carnera ("Babe") quickly became the light-heavyweight boxing champion in Iowa. "The best thing boxing does for you is give you a competitive spirit," Babe told Offenburger. "Brother, I'll tell you, you've got to be a competitor in life if you want to get anyplace."

After three years, Babe saw that there would never be much money in boxing. Professional wrestling provided an attractive option for Babe, a colorful character who could play to the crowds. Within three months of starting his wrestling career, Babe was competing in main events in Minneapolis. It wasn't long before he was starring in main events at Madison Square Garden in New York City.

As his wrestling career flourished in the next six years, he traveled from Toronto to Los Angeles and other cities, making a lot of money along the way. After he retired from wrestling, Babe and his young wife, Catherine, settled in Des Moines, where they raised their family of five children.

Babe also used the money he'd made as a wrestler (plus some additional loans) to open a tavern. It helped that he had $5,000 in his bank account by 1939 (that's more than $90,000 in today's dollars). Why a tavern? "Well, you'd have to have brains to be a plumber or electrician or something like that," Babe told Offenburger. "All I had was my name. I was well known from being in the ring."

Babe recalled how he had knelt down on the opening day of Babe's Tavern on March 25, 1939, to ask God "that I could sell one keg and ten cases of beer so I could clear the twenty-five dollars a day I needed to stay open." Babe, who was twenty-six at the time, not only managed to sell that much beer, but the tavern thrived as well. In 1941, he added a supper club on the second floor. Shortly thereafter, he added the Jungle Club as a special section, decorating it with bamboo and installing illegal but very popular slot machines.

The slot machines weren't the only attraction that helped business boom. Back then, there was no liquor by the drink in Iowa at restaurants. If restaurant patrons wanted a shot of real booze, they had to buy their own bottle and take it to a "key club," where they'd be charged for the mix, the glass and the ice.

Key clubs—country clubs, Elks clubs, American Legion halls and others— were allowed to set up lockers in which members could place bottles of alcohol purchased from the state liquor stores. Each member was given a key to a locker. When members would visit the establishment, they could take out their bottle of booze and consume alcohol on the premises. The establishment itself, however, could not legally supply liquor, either by the bottle or the glass.

Babe had a revelation when the fans of the St. Ambrose College football team came to town to watch their Fighting Bees play the Drake University Bulldogs.

"Keep in mind they came from Davenport, which is a Mississippi River town and was as wide open as river towns usually are for booze and stuff like that," Babe recalled. "They came in before the game and had some beers, but they really wanted booze. I told them I couldn't serve it."

The fans went out, bought six bottles of liquor and brought them back to Babe's. All he had to do was mix the drinks. "They [the fans] said they'd be back after the game and that I should just serve them drinks out of those bottles and charge them a regular price. Well, I did that, and I never saw so much money come into my cash register so quick and easy. I thought to myself, 'My God, where have I been?'"

Babe started selling booze illegally—even in coffee cups if heat from the cops was on—and his business soared. The biggest challenge was keeping the bar stocked. Babe smuggled in liquor from Minneapolis in trucks, hearses and any other conveyance he could think of, while his kitchen helpers bought as much as they could from Iowa state liquor stores without arousing too many suspicions, wrote the *Des Moines Register* in 1989.

To show how much Babe prospered in his own business during the war years, Babe's younger brother Chuck explained it best. When Chuck left Des Moines to serve in the military in 1944, Babe owed money on nine loans. When Chuck returned home two years later, Babe was more than a millionaire.

WACS MADE BABE'S THEIR UNOFFICIAL HEADQUARTERS

What really solidified Babe's success were the Women's Army Corps (WAC) members at Fort Des Moines who made Babe's their unofficial headquarters during World War II.

Following the attack on Pearl Harbor on December 7, 1941, Congress approved the creation of the Women's Army Auxiliary Corps (WAAC) on May 14, 1942. The first Officers Candidate School class was formed on July 20 that year.

Fort Des Moines was selected as the site of the first training center for the WAAC, which became WAC in 1943. More than thirty-five thousand women from all over the country applied for fewer than one thousand anticipated positions, according to the U.S. Army.

Fort Des Moines itself was as unique as the women who began training there in the summer of 1942. Located on the south edge of Iowa's capital city, Fort Des Moines (built in 1903) was one of the last and largest cavalry facilities constructed in the twentieth century, complete with a picturesque parade ground.

From 1942, when the first WAC officers were trained, to 1946, when the group was largely demobilized, more than 150,000 women served in the corps, noted the article "World War II: A Woman's Story," which ran in the *Stars and Stripes* newspaper in 2003. WACs were assigned to roles as clerks, typists, drivers, cooks and other noncombat duties that would "free a man to fight." The corps marked the beginning of a fully gender-integrated U.S. military.

During World War II, roughly seventy-two thousand women trained at Fort Des Moines, which had been hastily converted into headquarters and barracks for women in 1942. Despite the intensive use of disinfectants, everything still reeked of the horses that had recently been stabled there, noted the *Stars and Stripes*.

Since there were so many female recruits training at Fort Des Moines, not all of them could be housed at the fort. Some stayed at several downtown hotels, including the twelve-story Savery Hotel (now a boutique hotel known as the Renaissance Des Moines Savery Hotel at 401 Locust Street). The WACs and the Savery were featured in the 1945 movie *Keep Your Powder Dry*, starring Lana Turner, noted "Hotel Savery—Rich in Des Moines History," an article that appeared in the July 19, 2000 issue of the *Des Moines Register*.

The WACs were great for business in downtown Des Moines. "When the women were early in their training, they had to stay right there, but when

During World War II, roughly seventy-two thousand women trained at Fort Des Moines. The Women's Army Corps (WAC) members were great for business in downtown Des Moines, including Babe's restaurant. *Author's collection.*

they'd get their first night off, this town would be jumping," recalled Babe, who didn't serve in World War II because he was designated 4F (unfit for military service) due to his ulcers.

The presence of all those WACs in Des Moines "really made me," Babe said. His restaurant would sell more booze on a Saturday night back then than the place sold in a month by the 1980s. "I did my part [for the war effort]," Babe noted. "I kept an awful lot of them happy. None of them ever left my joint hungry or dry, just because they didn't happen to have any money."

THE GREAT UNDERWEAR DEBATE

Many of the WACs patronized Babe's during their time in Des Moines, not just to socialize, but for more basic reasons too. Odd as it might seem today, feminine clothing was a major preoccupation not only for the WACs but also for the general public, who were watching for any signs that the women were "masculizing" themselves in the military.

The WACs hated their army-issue khaki underwear and cotton (rather than nylon) stockings. "After a few months we were permitted to wear 'civilian' panties, to our great joy," recalled Doris (Brill) Mamolen, who arrived at Fort Des Moines after enlisting in the WAAC on October 14, 1942.

If the ladies at Fort Des Moines didn't have enough time to shop for clothes they needed, they'd leave an order with Babe, who would send one of his waitresses over to the Younkers department store at Seventh and Walnut Streets downtown to buy items like undergarments. They'd have them all ready to go the next time the WACs returned to Babe's restaurant.

The WACs always knew that they could count on Babe. While the WACs had to be back at Fort Des Moines by midnight and sometimes missed the last streetcar of the night running to that area, Babe would have one of his employees drive them back to Fort Des Moines in Babe's Cadillac.

The WACs appreciated this service. After the women completed their training at Fort Des Moines, Babe would receive pictures from all over the world where the WACs were stationed. "They'd put up signs in front of their commissary there calling it 'Babe's,' or they'd have a sign up saying it was so many miles to Babe's," he recalled.

This spread Babe's fame worldwide. Des Moines—which was booming with nightclubs, restaurants and other attractions during this era—was one of the hottest destinations in America in those often loose days of World War II, especially for military pilots.

"The boys would hear about the WACs and Des Moines, so they'd come here on furlough and stay here their whole furlough and not even get home," Babe told Offenburger. "There were so many women running around here that many of the air force pilots started having 'engine trouble' around Des Moines and would stay over two or three days here. The air force finally came close to putting the Des Moines Airport off limits because of that."

Many WACs recalled those days fondly. In the late 1980s, Offenburger interviewed Peggy Graffouliere—a former WAC who was eighty years old and living in the Carmel, California area—about her memories of Babe's. "Babe's was *the* place to go then," Peggy said. "The food was magnificent, the band was lovely, the place was beautifully decorated and there were those double bars. Yes, we all knew he [Babe] was selling booze illegally, but the laws were so stupid then I think everybody in Iowa got drunk on purpose. It was the drinkingest place I've ever seen." Peggy became such a regular, in fact, that she married Babe's bandleader, the late Armand "Frenchy" Graffouliere of Des Moines, a well-known pianist, organist and entertainer.

Speaking of entertainment, an eighteen-year-old freshman majoring in music at Drake University became a dinner hour piano player at Babe's during that era. In fact, Babe gave Louis Weertz, a Des Moines kid and son of a Lutheran pastor, his first professional job, paying him two dollars

Vintage matchbook covers tell Babe's story. After opening Babe's Tavern downtown on March 25, 1939, Babe added a restaurant and the Jungle Club with illegal slot machines. *Courtesy of Mike Avitt.*

per hour and all the spaghetti he could eat. Louis, better known as Roger Williams, went on to become one of the world's most famous pianists, with hits like "Autumn Leaves," "Born Free" and "The Impossible Dream."

As far as Babe was concerned, the greatest song Roger Williams ever played was a rollicking tune called "The Donkey Serenade." "There was something captivating about the way he played, even then," Babe told Offenburger. "People would really listen to him. And, God, I can remember one night when we got raided while he was playing, and he was so cool that he just kept playing while the police were running around getting the liquor and arresting people."

Brushes with the law were nothing new for Babe. It wasn't uncommon to see news item like this one from a July 1943 edition of the *Des Moines Tribune*: "Patrolman Mose Clayton came around the corner of Seventh Street and Grand Avenue at 1:20 a.m. Tuesday and found the operators of two top-flight nightclubs rolling around on the sidewalk, locked in combat." Turns out Babe had his arm around the neck of H. Ward Benson, operator of Benson's Dinner Club. Testimony in court indicated that Benson was at the Chesterfield Club when he saw Babe coming in. "There goes that guy who thinks he runs this town," Benson shouted. Babe allegedly walked over to Benson's table and said, "I understand you don't like this dago," referring to himself. Then Babe issued an invitation for Benson to join him on the street, where Patrolman Clayton found them brawling.

"The fascinating thing about Bisignano is that he has always been able to go so quickly from being perceived as a public brute—whether innocent or guilty—to being perceived as a saint of a man with the public's best interest and welfare beating foremost in his heart," Offenburger noted.

Consider February 1944. Less than a year after his brawl with Benson, Babe led an effort by twenty-five Des Moines tavern operators to sell war bonds. Babe, the former shoeshine boy, set up a shoeshine stand downtown, hired an orchestra to back him and had some of the wealthiest and most influential leaders of Des Moines coming by to get their shoes shined and make a donation. He raised $121,175 in a matter of hours. (That's more than $1.7 million in 2019 dollars.)

CHEF ROY HIESHIMA: FROM A JAPANESE RELOCATION CAMP TO BABE'S

When he wasn't fighting or fundraising, Babe was tending to business. Babe was a hard worker, often staying at the restaurant until 2:00 a.m. or 3:00 a.m. "I'm always running around with a towel and cleaning up the tables and taking dishes away," Babe told the local media. "That's why I got the nickname 'the millionaire busboy.'"

In 1944, he bought the building at 417 Sixth Avenue, where his downtown restaurant would flourish for generations. Along the way, he also bought Casson's meat market in Des Moines, mainly to ensure a good supply of quality meat during the years of war rationing.

The war had left no part of daily life untouched. That included Babe's business, which had become known as the swankiest nightclub in Des Moines with some of the best food in town. This was due, in part, to Roy Hieshima, a supervising chef at Babe's who had come to Des Moines in October 1943 from a Japanese relocation camp.

Hieshima was one of more than 120,000 West Coast residents with Japanese ancestry who were forced to leave their homes and jobs in World War II and move to one of ten isolated relocation centers in Arizona, Arkansas, California, Colorado, Idaho, Utah and Wyoming.

Following the Japanese attack on Pearl Harbor, Hawaii, on December 7, 1941, panicked people believed that every person of Japanese ancestry could be a potential spy, ready and willing to assist in an invasion of America. By February 1942, President Franklin D. Roosevelt had signed Executive Order 9066, authorizing specific areas within the United States as "military zones" in which Japanese Americans, regardless of their status of U.S. citizenship, were imprisoned without due process for the duration of the war.

Following the signing of Executive Order 9066, many Japanese Americans families were given less than two weeks' notice, sometimes less than one week, to vacate their homes and abandon their lives, according to the National Park Service (NPS). Immediately after the forced removal from their homes, they were held in temporary detention centers while "relocation centers" were under construction.

Roy Hieshima, who had lived in Los Angeles, California, was sent to the Jerome Relocation Center at Denson, Arkansas, before he came to Des Moines. The speed at which all this occurred was stunning. Construction began on July 15, 1942, for the Jerome Relocation Center, which opened in southeastern Arkansas on October 6, 1942. By November 1942, the Jerome Relocation Center's population had reached 8,497, as internees like Hieshima arrived from California and Hawaii.

Little is known about Hieshima's life before he came to the Jerome Relocation Center. History does record what life was like at the Jerome Relocation Center, which was located in the middle of heavily wooded swamp land in the Mississippi River Delta region. Life was difficult at Jerome due to the humidity and high rainfall, which made mud, mosquitoes, malaria and other maladies a constant threat.

The camp was divided into fifty blocks surrounded by a barbed wire fence, a patrol road and seven watch towers, noted the Japanese American Veterans Association. There were more than 610 buildings at the center, including administration areas, a hospital, residential barracks, elementary schools and a high school, a recreation building, a mess hall and a bathroom/laundry building.

The internees themselves provided much of the general labor, clearing land, digging ditches and building bridges. Because of drainage problems, an eight-mile canal was constructed that enabled them to run a successful farm operation. By 1943, 630 acres were under cultivation. The Jerome Relocation Center was able to grow 85 percent of its own vegetables. In addition, the internees raised more than 1,200 hogs for consumption at the camp.

While it's unclear exactly how Hieshima ended up in Des Moines, it was likely connected to an Application for Leave Clearance that was administered by the War Relocation Authority (WRA). The questions in this application

Roy Hieshima from California became a supervising chef at Babe's after coming to Des Moines in October 1943 from a Japanese relocation camp in Arkansas. *Courtesy of University of California–Berkeley.*

were designed to determine who was loyal to the United States. The WRA's leave clearance enabled many internees to resettle outside the relocation camps before the end of the war.

Hieshima made his way to Des Moines, where he landed a job cooking at Babe's restaurant. He lived at 2023 Grand Avenue in a boarding home operated by Mr. and Mrs. K. Minami, a Japanese couple who had been interned at the Minidoka Relocation Center near Hunt, Idaho.

While little is known about Hieshima or what became of him after his career at Babe's, the tradition of Japanese American cooks continued when Susie Kataoka joined the kitchen staff around 1953. When the *Des Moines Tribune* announced its "Polk County Pizza Champs" in September 1970, Babe's made the top five, thanks to "Japanese-American Susie Kataoka, who has been making Italian pizza in the front window of the downtown restaurant for 17 years." She made more than 100,000 pizzas in 1969, noted the 1970 newspaper article.

BUSTED!

Long before Babe's was winning pizza awards, however, Babe himself was making headlines, not for his restaurant's food, but rather his brushes with the law. After World War II ended, Des Moines city leaders and local politicians made a concerted effort to clean up the city, taking aim at gambling dens and liquor sellers. As the city's largest and best-known tavern/restaurant, Babe's was a natural target.

Babe's was closed for most of 1947, when Babe spent six months in jail for his shenanigans regarding illegal liquor sales. While his restaurant was padlocked, he worked out a deal so the local Alcoholics Anonymous chapter could use it for its meetings. "The place where these same people used to go to get loaded, now they used it to cure themselves of their sickness," Babe told *Des Moines* magazine in 1986. "It worked out very well for both of us."

Babe's exploits at this time were among the most covered events in Des Moines media history, noted Offenburger, a longtime columnist for the *Des Moines Register*. "Keep in mind that by then, Babe was a man who was getting more press than the governor of Iowa [Robert Blue, a Republican from Eagle Grove], and here Babe was going to the calaboose."

Babe's exploits made headlines in newspapers across the state, from the *Sioux City Journal* and the *Council Bluffs Nonpareil* in the west to the *Muscatine Journal* and *Waterloo Courier* in eastern Iowa. "The 100 prisoners in the county jail have profited from Bisignano's confinement," according to a March 1947 *Des Moines Tribune* article that detailed Babe's immense popularity. "The bulk of the weekly delivery of boxes and baskets of fruit, candy and tobacco from Bisignano's friends is divided up on Bisignano's direction for distribution to the other prisoners. Thursday, visiting day, about 60 persons visited Bisignano at the jail."

It's amazing they could find him at the jail, because he wasn't there all that much. During the day, he essentially had a work-release program where he was a groundskeeper at the county juvenile home. Babe found out the juvenile home wasn't buying meat from Casson's, the meat market he owned. "I sold them on buying meat from me," Babe said.

Babe even had a deal at night where he'd go home until about 4:00 a.m., and then the jailers would sneak him back into the jail. The night before his sentence expired, Babe threw a farewell banquet for the inmates and jailers, with all the food and drink catered in. There's an outrageous photo of the whole group with their arms draped over one another's shoulders as they stand in front of a table loaded with food.

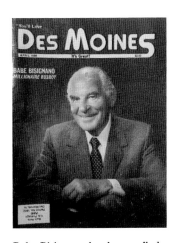

"The Babe Bisignano Show, I've called it," Offenburger wrote. "And as it plays on, it's hard to know whether to call it a comedy or a tragedy. Higher highs and lower lows than normally exist in several lifetimes all come to play in the singular life of this simple, yet complex, man."

Babe's colorful personality made him a natural when he played the slick, rough-talking gambler "Big Jule" in the Des Moines Community Playhouse's 1958 production of *Guys and Dolls*. Crowds packed the theater, and the musical's run was extended to accommodate everyone who wanted to see the show. Theater fit Babe's style perfectly.

Babe Bisignano has been called "the best-known character in Iowa and beyond." In April 1986, *Des Moines* magazine ran the cover story "Babe Bisignano: Millionaire Bus Boy." *Courtesy of Italian American Heritage Center.*

"Nobody knows how to work with the public better than me," Babe told Offenburger. "When people come in [to my restaurant], they know that sooner or later I'm going to drop by their table and talk to them, buy them a drink, whatever. Yeah, I'm on stage every night."

A TOUGH EXTERIOR CONCEALED A KIND HEART

Babe's celebrity never waned. When city leaders and real estate developers were talking about a big building project for downtown Des Moines, the catch was that the city would have to condemn Babe's restaurant so they could get the land. Businessman Bill Knapp was quoted in the local paper saying, "It'd be easier to condemn the state capitol than it would be to condemn Babe's restaurant." "I liked that," Babe said.

Children who visited Babe's restaurant with their parents often received a "Babe's My Pal" button or balloon. When a group of 1980s professional

When a group of 1980s professional wrestling stars, including Hulk Hogan, performed in Des Moines, they celebrated with a dinner at Babe's restaurant. Babe and the Hulk were photographed together. Babe handed out hundreds of copies of that photo to friends and guests at the restaurant, especially kids, always signing them, "I'm the one on the left." *Author's collection.*

wrestling stars, including Hulk Hogan, performed in Des Moines, they celebrated with a dinner at Babe's restaurant. Babe and the Hulk were photographed together. Babe handed out hundreds of copies of that photo to friends and guests at the restaurant, especially kids.

Babe, partly because of his celebrity, became the most famous (or at least the most readily identifiable) Italian in Iowa, Offenburger noted. In the 1980s, a third-grade teacher from the southwest Iowa town of Creston wrote to Babe, telling him that her students were studying Italy, and there were no Italian people around for them to talk to. She wondered if Babe might come to Creston give a program on his ethnicity for her class. Babe did better than that. He brought the whole class to Des Moines for a pizza party at his restaurant and then regaled them with stories about his Italian heritage, Offenburger noted.

Babe exhibited a sense of caring for others, especially those who were less fortunate. On cold winter nights, he was known to invite a "half-frozen bum" off the street, sit him down next to the pizza ovens for a few minutes to help the man warm up and then give him a prime rib dinner.

Why did Babe want to help others? "Because I was so poor myself when I grew up—I mean really poor," he said. "I can remember so well when streetcar tickets were two for a nickel, and hell, I was still walking."

Babe also gave back to the community in many other ways. He helped found Big Brothers of Des Moines. *Des Moines* magazine noted in 1986 that the Babe Bisignano/Mercy Hospital Golf Classic earned $20,000 in 1985 (nearly $48,000 in today's dollars) for the drug and alcohol abuse programs of the Variety Club, a Des Moines–area charity dedicated to improving the lives of children who are at-risk, underprivileged, critically ill or living with special needs.

As Babe grew older, it became clear that the future of Babe's restaurant was uncertain. It was hard for the next generation to carry on the business, partly because Babe's children had other interests and partly because Babe's restaurant was really Babe himself.

In the fall of 1988, when Babe was seventy-five years old, he did something that everyone in town thought was crazy: he opened Babe's North, a smaller, more intimate version of his legendary downtown operation. "The real reason I did it is that I stayed downtown five years too long," Babe told Offenburger. "Nobody comes downtown anymore. If it wasn't for conventions coming into town, I couldn't exist downtown today."

As the fiftieth anniversary of Babe's restaurant approached, the local news covered the big event. "Babe Bisignano says the party he's throwing at his place next Saturday night is going to be the biggest bash the venerable old joint has seen since World War II ended," noted the feature story "Babe, You've Got What It Takes," which appeared in the March 19, 1989 issue of the *Des Moines Register*.

The public was encouraged to attend to the celebration, which promised free beer, a band and games from 5:00 p.m. until everyone was ready to go home. Babe invited any veteran who could still get into his (or her) World War II uniform to eat and drink free of charge. Babe welcomed all of Iowa to the celebration, and most of them showed up, judging by downtown traffic on Sixth Avenue the evening of the party, according to news reports.

Revelers were packed shoulder-to-shoulder in all three dining rooms. Two six-foot television screens were brought in for those who couldn't see the stage, where Iowa native Roger Williams played the piano. "Even Horatio Alger, the master of rags-to-riches tales, couldn't have written a better final chapter than the one Babe staged last night," stated the *Des Moines Register*. "The party may also be something of a last hurrah for what is arguably the most famous bar, restaurant, dance hall and former bootlegging joint Iowa has ever known," added the *Register*. "But when Babe's does close, Des Moines and Iowa will be disconnected from a remarkable era."

Babe felt the same way. "If the day comes when there is no Babe's downtown, there will be an emptiness that will never be filled," said Babe, who closed his restaurant permanently in 1996.

After Babe died in 2005 at age ninety-two, the April 20, 2005 edition of the *Des Moines Register* included the article "Everyone Has a Story at Babe's Visitation." "The curtain comes down," said Reverend James Polich, pastor of St. Augustin's Catholic Church. "It's the end of a life, a dazzling and well-done performance that deserves applause."

Minestrone

This recipe is adapted from Babe Bisignano's book, *Cooking the Italian Way*, published in 2002. Minestrone is a rich, thick Italian soup made with fresh vegetables, often with the addition of pasta. Minestrone was originally a humble dish, made primarily with leftovers and intended for everyday consumption, since it was filling, inexpensive and good. There is not a set recipe for minestrone, since it is usually made out of whatever vegetables are in season.

1 16-ounce can kidney beans
1 clove garlic, minced
½ teaspoon salt
¼ teaspoon pepper
1 tablespoon olive oil
¼ cup chopped fresh parsley
2½ cups water
1 teaspoon basil
1 teaspoon oregano
1 small, fresh zucchini, unpeeled and diced
2 celery stalks, chopped
2 small carrots, peeled and diced
1 small onion, minced
1 16-ounce can crushed tomatoes
⅓ cup elbow macaroni, uncooked
½ cup beef bouillon or tomato juice
salt to taste

Put kidney beans in a large kettle and mash them slightly with a fork. Add garlic, salt, pepper, olive oil and parsley. Stir well. Add water, basil, oregano and all vegetables to the kettle. Bring soup to a boil over medium heat, stirring occasionally. Lower heat, cover the kettle and simmer 1 hour, stirring occasionally. After 1 hour, add macaroni and beef bouillon or tomato juice. Simmer 15 minutes, stirring occasionally. Add more salt to taste.

CHAPTER 4

Fine Dining in Des Moines

Steakhouses, Supper Clubs and Steak de Burgo

Ask someone who was raised in the 1950s in Iowa about dining in restaurants, especially the more upscale places, and you're likely to get an answer like this: "When I was a kid, going out to dinner was something only for a special occasion. Even going to a fast-food restaurant was something memorable back then."

Since many families were one-income households (almost always from the man's income), most people didn't have a lot of disposable income for eating out. Those were also the days when most families only had one car, one television set and one landline telephone. "I came from a family of eight children, so we didn't eat out much," recalled Lisa (Lamberto) Albright, who grew up in Des Moines and now lives on a farm near Lytton, Iowa. "Even McDonalds and pizza were a special treat."

Albright's father, Nick Lamberto, went out to eat during his workday. "My dad was a reporter for the *Des Moines Register*, and he would meet his cronies at Babe's restaurant downtown daily for lunch," she recalled.

For most people, taking the family out to lunch or dinner wasn't a daily or even weekly occurrence. Eating out in the 1950s and 1960s often meant celebrating an anniversary or birthday. The destination of choice tended to be a steakhouse or supper club, the kind of place where you'd dress up for a nice evening out.

Des Moines offered an excellent selection of these restaurants, especially on Fleur Drive. "Long-time Des Moines residents will remember Fleur Drive as the city's posh dining destination," noted the article "Fleur Drive

Steakhouses and supper clubs in Des Moines often offered classic ice cream cocktails. You can still get Grasshoppers at Jesse's Embers, which has served Des Moines since 1963. *Author's collection.*

to See Wave of New Businesses," which ran in the July 21, 2016 edition of the *Des Moines Register*. "Before the suburbs boomed and before downtown's recent resurgence, Fleur was the place to go for a nice meal."

Some of Des Moines's restaurants in this area were known for their fantastic buffets, like the Crystal Tree Restaurant and Lounge, which opened at 6111 South Fleur Drive in March 1977 to rave reviews. Guests could also enjoy Iowa classics like Stuffed Pork Chops, as well as more exotic fare like Roast Long Island Duckling, from the menu. The Crystal Tree, located at the Holiday Inn Airport, became a popular destination for high schoolers to take their prom dates.

The Pier on Fleur Drive mixed the atmosphere of a midwestern supper club with a nautical flair, thanks to the rope rails and wooden pier out front. This popular restaurant included a bar with a cozy fireplace. The Pier offered seafood items that were relatively unique for Iowa in the 1970s, including red snapper, orange roughy, giant tiger shrimp, clam stew and more, along with surf-and-turf options.

If you wanted a more traditional supper club or steakhouse experience, Des Moines was the place to be. Most of these restaurants had been in business for decades. Many were only open for supper. Nearly all were family owned and operated. Fine dining at these supper clubs and steakhouses in Des Moines meant good service and generous portions of prime rib, a baked potato and a stiff cocktail.

As you relaxed in this comfortable setting, which often included live music, you might finish off your meal with a classic ice cream cocktail like a Grasshopper.

Grasshopper Ice Cream Cocktail

1 shot green crème de menthe
1 shot white crème de cacao
2 scoops vanilla ice cream
fresh mint sprig, for garnish

Pour crème de menthe, crème de cacao and ice cream into a blender. Blend until thick and creamy. (To make this a little more thick and creamy, try adding 2 ice cubes and about 2 tablespoons of half and half.) Pour into a 12-ounce glass. Garnish with a sprig of mint.

JOHNNY AND KAY'S

Perhaps the most famous restaurant on Fleur Drive in years past was Johnny and Kay's. Johnny and Kay Compiano, a husband-and-wife team, opened this still-missed eatery near the Des Moines Municipal Airport at the intersection of Fleur Drive and Leland Avenue in 1946.

After graduating from North High in 1938, Kay met her husband of forty-two years, Johnny Compiano, at the Hotel Kirkwood in Des Moines, where she played the piano in the lounge and Johnny worked as a bellhop. After the couple married, they used Johnny's mustering-out pay and savings from his service in the U.S. Coast Guard to start their first restaurant while they were still in their twenties. Johnny and Kay's was a one-room restaurant and bar, essentially a roadside tavern, that could accommodate thirty-two people. "It was a little beer joint," Johnny told the *Des Moines Register* years ago. "We painted it, made curtains and got a little credit from Sears, Roebuck and Co., and others."

The small business grew to become one of the best-known eateries in central Iowa, complete with white tablecloth dining. Johnny and Kay's eventually became an Iowa landmark restaurant/hotel complex, with nine dining rooms and seating for 450 people. "We lived, ate and breathed our business," Kay Compiano told the *Des Moines Register*. "You would always find one of us there."

People still talk about Johnny and Kay's hand-cut steaks, from their celebrated Steak de Burgo to prime rib to filet mignon. Kay Compiano recalled how no detail escaped her husband's watchful eye as he managed the staff. "He would say, 'I've got to tell them they're putting too much juice on the prime rib,'" she said. "I'd tell him, 'You just keep still.'"

Other unforgettable foods at Johnny and Kay's included the three-tiered relish tray (with pickled herring); antipasto and salads with Kay's own recipes, including creamy Parmesan dressing; deep-fried shrimp; ribs and French dip sandwiches; French fried onion rings; fried chicken; red cake with white frosting; and an array of pies, from lime chiffon to strawberry to French silk.

Author Bill Bryson heard reports when he was growing up in the 1950s in Des Moines that Johnny and Kay's had the smoothest, most mouth-pleasing cheesecake around, "although my father was much too ill-at-ease with quality, and far too careful with his money, ever to take us to that outpost of fine dining on Fleur Drive," he wrote in his memoir *The Life and Times of the Thunderbolt Kid*.

Along with memories of the famous Sunday brunch, "phenomenal food" is a comment that comes up frequently on the "Lost Des Moines" Facebook

Johnny and Kay's restaurant offered live music. Co-owner Kay Compiano played the piano and sang on Friday and Saturday nights. She would take as many as one hundred requests for songs per evening. *Courtesy of Italian American Heritage Center.*

page when Johnny and Kay's is mentioned. People describe Johnny and Kay's as "the best of the best" and "a magical place."

"In those days, Johnny and Kay's was like the 801 Chophouse is today," said Connie Wimer, owner and chairman of Business Publications in Des Moines, referring to the upscale restaurant in downtown Des Moines known for its exceptional food and beverages.

Some people remembered the live music at Johnny and Kay's, where Kay played the piano and sang on Friday and Saturday nights. She would take as many as one hundred requests for songs per evening, noted her obituary in 2016. It seemed that nearly every teenager on Des Moines's south side worked there at one time or another. "The waiters were the best," is a common refrain for those who remember Johnny and Kay's.

The exceptional food and excellent service attracted a wide clientele to Johnny and Kay's. "My father was a business executive for Meredith Publishing, and he would entertain business associates at Johnny and Kay's after his seminars on using rotogravure printing presses for color printing

Johnny Compiano hand-cut the steaks for his restaurant on Fleur Drive. People still talk about the great steaks at Johnny and Kay's, from Steak de Burgo to prime rib to filet mignon. *Courtesy of Italian American Heritage Center.*

enhancement," said Billie (McKowen) Bergquist, who graduated from Abraham Lincoln High School in Des Moines in 1966 and now lives near Lohrville, Iowa. "The aged steaks, salad with homemade Roquefort dressing and Italian spumoni ice cream dessert made for a fine meal."

Those were the days before liquor by the drink could be sold at Iowa restaurants. "Father kept a large liquor locker that held popular and expensive brands in order to provide for his business associates," Bergquist said. "Each bottle had a special sticker from the State of Iowa designating use by personal locker only."

In 1934, Iowa became one of the original "control" or "monopoly" states following the repeal of national Prohibition in 1933. The state assumed direct control over the wholesale and retail distribution of all alcoholic beverages, except beer. It wasn't until 1963 that the Class C liquor license was created, allowing the sale of alcoholic beverages by the drink for on-premises consumption.

Johnny and Kay sold their restaurant to the Hyatt House hotel chain in 1968 after Johnny suffered a series of heart attacks, according to the *Des Moines Register*. Five years later, the Compianos opened the Poppin' Fresh Pies restaurant at 4107 Merle Hay Road in Des Moines. They later joined the Pillsbury Corporation, which was developing plans for a chain of similar restaurants at the time.

After the Compianos sold their minority interest in the chain in 1976, Johnny stayed on as a consultant. "The Poppin' Fresh name appeared on restaurants in the East and Middle West, as well as on Pillsbury ready-to-bake products," noted the article "Des Moines Restauranteur John Compiano Dies at 63," which appeared in the February 2, 1984 issue of the *Des Moines Register*. "The restaurant chain recently was sold, and the stores were renamed Bakers Square restaurant and pie shops."

No matter what restaurant business they were in, it was never just a job for Johnny and Kay. "I guess you start out in this business for financial reasons," Johnny Compiano told the *Des Moines Register*. "You end up doing it for love."

Johnny and Kay's Salad Dressing

This recipe turns up from time to time on various Facebook groups related to Des Moines history.

1 cup sour cream
1 cup mayonnaise
1 teaspoon garlic salt
1 tablespoon lemon juice
½ tablespoon anchovy paste
¼ cup grated Romano cheese
¼ cup grated Parmesan cheese
1 teaspoon paprika
1 teaspoon granulated sugar

Combine all ingredients in blender or food processor. Cover and chill mixture for 24 hours before serving.

STEAK DE BURGO: A DES MOINES CLASSIC

Of all the exceptional food served at Johnny and Kay's, perhaps nothing lives on like Steak de Burgo. This regional specialty is a traditional, hearty steak dish—usually made with a beef tenderloin—topped with butter, Italian herbs and garlic.

The history of Steak de Burgo, which is virtually unheard of outside of central Iowa, goes back decades. A 1964 *Better Homes and Gardens* cookbook titled *Famous Food from Famous Places* listed Steak de Burgo as a specialty of the house at Johnny and Kay's Restaurant. Tom Compiano, son of Johnny and Kay, said his father brought the recipe up from New Orleans, where he was stationed during World War II. When he opened Johnny and Kay's in 1946, it became a popular house specialty, according to information from the Iowa Beef Industry Council.

Compiano added that chefs who worked for his father would often take the recipe with them when they opened places of their own. Hence, the proliferation of Steak de Burgo in Des Moines, the theory goes. Steak de

Burgo can still be found on many Des Moines restaurants' menus, from Tursi's Latin King to Johnny's Italian Steakhouse. "People love Steak de Burgo," said Bob Tursi, owner of Tursi's Latin King. "It's a Des Moines acquired taste."

Des Moines's signature dish always begins the same way—with a great quality piece of tenderloin. While it's incredibly tender, it's not the most flavorful. That's where the additional ingredients come in. It's also where the agreement ends on what defines Steak de Burgo. Cooks include everything from garlic butter to oregano to heavy cream to seasoning salt to vermouth to give the tender, melt-in-your-mouth beef the distinctive Steak de Burgo flair.

Chef George Formaro, a Des Moines native, shared a recipe for his version that pays homage to the flavors of the classic Steak de Burgo. This is the garlic butter and herb version, said George, who emphasized that Iowa beef makes a huge difference.

Steak de Burgo

Spice Mix
1 ½ tablespoons dried basil
1 ½ tablespoons dried thyme
2 teaspoons oregano

4 8-ounce beef tenderloin steaks
2 tablespoons canola oil

1 tablespoon chopped garlic
1 tablespoon chopped shallots
1 stick butter
salt and pepper, to taste

Mix spice blend. Season tenderloin steaks with salt and pepper. Coat steaks with spice blend. Save the remaining herbs to season vegetables.
Heat sauté pan over medium-high heat. Add canola oil. When oil has heated, add seasoned tenderloin steaks to the pan. Flip the meat over when the bottom side has browned nicely. Continue to cook on other side until desired temperature is reached. (Do yourself a favor

and use a meat thermometer. Do not cook over 145 degrees. Aim for 125 degrees for rare, 135 degrees for medium rare and 145 for medium doneness.)

Remove beef from pan and set aside. In the same pan, add garlic, shallots and butter. Shake pan back and forth until butter is melted. Season with salt and pepper to taste. Pour garlic butter sauce over beef tenderloins and serve.

JOHNNY'S VET'S CLUB

Steak de Burgo was always a favorite at Johnny's Vet's Club. In 1946, John Stamatelos converted a Valley Junction home at the corner of Sixty-Third Street and Railroad Avenue into a supper club that became a popular destination for decades. "Back when it opened, it was kind of like a speakeasy," said Darren Brown, who grew up in the area and runs Nostalgic Enterprises, a classic car shop in Valley Junction in West Des Moines.

The back room housed the bar, while the dining room was up front, recalled longtime Des Moines resident Connie Wimer. The one-story building was dark and smoky, with low ceilings and a red lightbulb inside the front door. "It had a gritty feel, almost like something out of a Martin Scorsese film, but the food was awesome," said Brown, whose parents took him there occasionally when he was growing up. "Before the 801 Chophouse opened downtown, this was where big-name local businessmen like the Ruans and the Hubbells would meet."

When you stepped into the tiny entry area, there sat Johnny Stamatelos to greet you, noted the blog *Dennis: Now and Ago*. "My dad and mom loved going to Johnny's Vet's Club every Saturday night," recalled Des Moines native Lisa (Lamberto) Albright of Lytton. "They always had a table reserved for them."

People enjoyed the casual atmosphere and great food, including Steak de Burgo, pasta dishes and top sirloin served on a metal plate with a small stick noting whether the meat was prepared rare, medium rare or well done.

After Albright and her husband, Alan, married, they occasionally joined her parents for dinner at Johnny's Vet's Club. "Alan is a cattle producer, so he likes supporting a good steakhouse," said Albright, who added that Johnny's Vet's Club always had the best Greek salads.

Due to its location in a low-lying area on the south edge of Valley Junction, not far from the Raccoon River, Johnny's Vet's Club was prone to flooding. When the old-time supper club was forced to close after the massive 1993 flood, Iowa restaurateur Mike Whalen carried on the name and tradition of Johnny's Vet's Club through Johnny's Italian Steakhouse, a restaurant franchise with locations in Des Moines, Altoona and beyond.

No matter what you eat at Johnny's today, there's one guiding philosophy that carries over from the Johnny's Vet's Club days, Whalen said. "A great steak is the measure of a true Midwest meal."

ROCKY'S, WIMPY'S, VIC'S TALLY HO AND THE SILHOUETTE

Great steaks were the order of the day at Rocky's Steak House, established at Fleur Drive and Stanton Avenue around 1939 by Rocky Compiano.

Operated out of a former farmhouse, Rocky's (later known as Rocky's White Shutter Inn) offered steakhouse fare, seafood, cocktails and even Cantonese food, all served in four elegant alcoves. The restaurant, which was open six days a week (closed Sundays) from 5:00 p.m. to 1:00 a.m., was later converted into Fatino's Italian-American Cucina.

Another south side favorite was Wimpy's Steak House at 1604 South Union Street, owned by Joe "Wimpy" Cimino. Wimpy's became a Des Moines institution for nearly fifty years, opening in 1931 and closing in 1980. Cimino, who originally sold large hamburgers for a nickel, lived above the restaurant.

Wimpy's specialized in prime rib, steaks, fried chicken and "fish the way you like it," according to its advertisements, which encouraged people to "Bring the Family." Unlike other steakhouses and supper clubs in Des Moines, which were only open in the evening, Wimpy's served from 8:00 a.m. to 11:00 p.m. every weekday, Saturdays from 8:00 a.m. to midnight and was closed Sundays. "We went there for lunch mostly," Wimer said. "It was an elegant place with all-male waiters."

Cimino often hired men released from the city and county jail to give them a new start in life. These servers were known for taking accurate orders for large parties using only their memories.

Woody Bell of Des Moines remembered delivering three-hundred-gallon barrels of vinegar to Wimpy's. "Employees used the vinegar to wipe down and sanitize the dining tables," said Bell, who started working in 1957 as

Left: Terrific steaks were the order of the day at Rocky's Steak House, established at Fleur Drive and Stanton Avenue around 1939 by Rocky Compiano. *Courtesy of Italian American Heritage Center.*

Below: Wimpy's Steak House at 1604 South Union Street was owned by Joe "Wimpy" Cimino. Wimpy's opened in 1931 and closed in 1980. *Courtesy of Italian American Heritage Center.*

a delivery driver for the Hoxie Fruit and Produce Company, which later became part of the Sysco Corporation.

Fine dining restaurants could also be found in the area where Merle Hay Mall opened in 1959. Vic and Mary Talerico operated Vic's Tally Ho at 5601 Douglas Avenue (at the corner of Fifty-Sixth Street). After opening in 1940, Vic's Tally Ho became the place to go for steaks, deep-fried shrimp and more. Vic Talerico made the local news when he was the high bidder for the Grand Champion Beef Carcass at the 1960 Iowa State Fair.

Vic's Tally Ho became a favorite destination for people celebrating special events, including anniversaries, birthdays and prom dates. Besides the great food, Vic's Tally Ho was noted for live jazz from talented performers like Ernest "Speck" Redd, the top jazz pianist in Des Moines. Fans loved his showy, improvisational style.

While fire destroyed the original building in 1962, Vic's reopened a year later with much fanfare. After Talerico passed away in 1971, the restaurant (which was called Mr. Vic's by then) closed permanently in 1974.

The legacy of Vic's Tally Ho lives on. "I always remember the advice Vic gave me as a teen," said Steve Lyle, a former employee who shared his memories of working at the restaurant in a post on the "Lost Des Moines" Facebook page. "He said save a nickel from every dollar you earn, and you'll

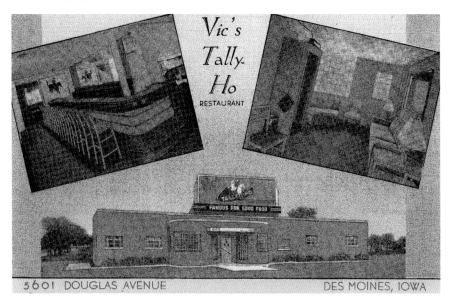

Vic and Mary Talerico operated Vic's Tally Ho at 5601 Douglas Avenue. After opening in 1940, Vic's Tally Ho became the place to go for steaks, deep-fried shrimp and more. *Author's collection.*

The Silhouette Restaurant became synonymous with dinner after church. While there was often a line of people on the porch waiting to get into the farmhouse turned restaurant at the intersection of Douglas Avenue and Merle Hay Road, guests agreed that the food was worth the wait. *Author's collection.*

end up a millionaire. Although I'm not rich, I am much better off having tried to follow his advice."

Not far from Vic's Tally Ho was the Silhouette Restaurant, which became synonymous with dinner after church. While there would often be a line of people on the porch of this farmhouse turned restaurant, the food was worth the wait, recalled loyal customers. From the mid-1950s to 1970, the Silhouette satisfied families who enjoyed old-fashioned comfort food like fried chicken, Swiss steak with tomato gravy, chicken and dumplings, prime rib and other signature dishes.

The Silhouette, which was located at the intersection of Douglas Avenue and Merle Hay Road, was owned by Mary and Fred Wall, who also owned and operated four other now-closed restaurants, including The Inn on Delaware and Hi-Ho Grill.

Swiss Steak and Tomato Gravy

In the November 1, 1995 edition of the *Des Moines Register*, Mary Wall shared this recipe from the Silhouette. The recipe is in restaurant proportions.

1 No. 10 can tomatoes (roughly 12¾ cups)
2 cups water
1 medium onion, chopped
6 stalks celery, chopped
½ green pepper

1 tablespoon sugar
2 tablespoons salt
½ teaspoon pepper
1 teaspoon chili powder
1 teaspoon garlic powder
1 quart leftover (or canned) beef gravy

Brown the Swiss steak and put in a pan with tomato gravy mixture. Cook in a covered pan slowly for 2 to 3 hours or until meat is tender. (Notice that this recipe is fairly vague by today's standards. It doesn't list what beef cut to use. Round steak is typically used in Swiss steak, usually 2 to 2.5 pounds for 4 to 6 servings. To make the tomato gravy, combine all the ingredients listed in the recipe. After putting the round steak and the tomato gravy in a pan, cover the pan with a tight-fitting lid. Bring the steak in the tomato purée to a simmer and then maintain a low simmer.)

GINO'S COMBINED ITALIAN STYLE WITH STEAKHOUSE SIZZLE

Steaks with Italian flair were a big part of Gino's Restaurant & Lounge, located at 2809 Sixth Avenue in Des Moines. "Almost every time I go to review an old-line place that's packed with regulars every weekend, I end up sorely disappointed and add to my already long list of enemies," wrote J.R. Miller in "Everyone Loves Gino's and with Good Reason," which appeared in the January 1998 edition of the *Datebook Diner*. "It didn't take many weeks on this job to discover that just because everyone in the world eats somewhere once a week doesn't mean it's good. This time the masses have been vindicated."

Gino's was well known for its corn-fed steak, noted a 2011 entry in the blog *Distilled Opinion: Iowa Opinions About Food and Drink*. "The steak is usually the best steak to be found anywhere in Iowa."

Gino's owner, Gino Foggia, a Des Moines native, paid his dues working fifteen years at Johnny and Kay's, including ten years as its executive chef. In 1966, Foggia bought the Chickadee Restaurant from Larry and Carolyn Marxer. The Marxers had operated the Chickadee since 1928.

In 1966, Gino Foggia bought the Chickadee Restaurant, which had served Des Moines since 1928. Steaks with an Italian flair defined Gino's Restaurant & Lounge at 2809 Sixth Avenue. *Courtesy of Italian American Heritage Center.*

Foggia advertised this as the longest tenure of a restaurant at one location in Des Moines. For years, an old Chickadee Restaurant menu displayed on the wall of the entry to Gino's proclaimed, "On the wrong side of: the fence, the tracks, the river, the hill town. The food must be good."

Ginos' developed a well-earned reputation as a steakhouse, known for its juicy New York strip streaks and its famous Steak de Burgo. In a 2006 interview with the *Des Moines Register*, Foggia explained the history of his style of Steak de Burgo: "I originally worked at Johnny and Kay's for 15 years. That's where that Steak de Burgo originated, and I brought it back with me." Gino's was also known for its famous Italian Fried Chicken, with its crisp coating spiced with parsley, oregano and cheese covering juicy meat.

With its comfortable, Naugahyde-style cushioned booths, friendly service and traditional Italian American menu, Gino's was the kind of casual place you could count on to make you feel at home. "The quiet hum of Gino's always-large crowd is peaceful and relaxing," noted the *Datebook Diner* in 1995.

While the restaurant's interior was generally red, dim and wood-grained Formica, the food and the service were "worthy of linen, Haviland [china dishes] and armloads of expensive flowers," Miller wrote. "Whatever you do, do the toasted ravioli," Miller added. "I don't even like ravioli very much, but the wonderfully flavored meat filling and the greaseless, crunchy brown pasta surrounding it won my heart."

Through the years, the building that first housed the Chickadee and later Gino's was remodeled numerous times. By the early 1980s, Gino's could seat 175 guests, with 75 in the lounge. It opened at 4:30 p.m. for dinner. When asked why Gino's wasn't open for lunch, Foggia offered a simple answer in a 2006 interview with the *Des Moines Register*. "We use our kitchen during the day. We buy very few frozen items," said Foggia, who also opened Papa Gino's off Interstate 235 at Twenty-Second Street in West Des Moines in the early 1980s. "We make everything ourselves, and we cook to order a lot."

Gino's was known for good food at fair prices. "Apparently the recession has hit Gino's," wrote J.R. Miller in the *Datebook Diner* published in the *Des Moines Register* on December 12, 1991. "The printed prices on the menu, at least at the Sixth Avenue location, have been crossed out, and new, lower prices have been penciled in. Gino's was a bargain before and is even more so now." While Miller didn't specify exactly how much prices had been lowered, the article did note that entrées ranged from about $4.95 to $18.95.

Food writers of the era also commented on lasagna at Gino's. Unlike the typical layered affair of wide noodles, sauce and cheese, Gino's lasagna was a casserole of rigatoni, hardboiled eggs, meatballs, sauce and lots of cheese. "Despite the particular moniker, Gino's 'lasagna' is quite tasty," Miller wrote in the *Datebook Diner* in 1991.

These traditions that were unique to Gino's seemed to give the restaurant a timeless quality. Even the staff stayed the same at Gino's. "One waitress has worked at Gino's for 39 years," noted "Gino's Reputation Rests on Fresh Food, Consistency," which appeared in the April 13, 2006 issue of the *Des Moines Register*. "A bartender has worked there 27 years. Two cooks have each logged more than 20 years in the kitchen. Good people are key ingredients for good food, owner Gino Foggia said."

All good things must end, though, including Gino's, which closed in 2015. When asked about the key to staying in business so long, Foggia was concise: "Consistency and service. That's about it."

IMAGINATION TOOK FLIGHT IN THE CLOUD ROOM

When you think of elegant dining in Des Moines, the airport probably isn't the first place that springs to mind, but things were different decades ago, especially when air travel was still a rarity. "Would you believe people used to go to airports just to eat food? Just for fun?" asked the 2014 Citylab.com article "When People Looked Forward to Eating Airport Food."

To understand why, realize that air travel in the 1950s and into the 1960s was still an upstart new technology, one that badly needed market share. In 1965, a full three decades after the advent of commercial flight, TIME magazine noted that eight in ten Americans had never been on a plane before. (Compare that to 2000, when half of Americans took at least one round-trip per year.)

A 1940s guide to commercial air transportation advised that good airports should have a "high-class waiting room, ticketing and restaurant facilities" to attract passengers who might otherwise opt for a train, noted the Citylab article.

Why "high-class?" In the 1950s and 1960s, U.S. domestic travelers could expect to pay 40 percent more per round-trip ticket than they do today,

By the 1960s, Des Moines's Cloud Room was billing itself as "Iowa's Family Eating Place." Postcards listed the restaurant at "Airport Terminal Building Des Moines 21, Iowa." *Author's collection.*

which meant flying was often the province of the well-to-do. Airports were encouraged to appeal to non-passengers, including the general public and sightseers, who might become new passengers.

It turns out that wasn't so difficult. By the 1950s, airports were not just travel hubs but something like tourist attractions. People sometimes came to the airport just to watch planes take off and land.

Des Moines's airport capitalized on this with its Cloud Room restaurant, which offered white tablecloth dining. Large windows filled the spacious dining room with natural light, offering good views of airplanes as they landed and departed.

The Cloud Room, which billed itself as "Iowa's Family Eating Place," listed its location as "Airport Terminal Building Des Moines 21, Iowa." By the 1970s, however, the heyday of destination airport restaurants was over. The novelty had worn off, especially as air travel became increasingly common for the masses.

HOLIDAY INN PUT A NEW SPIN ON DINING

Perhaps no restaurant in Des Moines offered a more unique ambiance than the Top O' the Tower at the Holiday Inn (now known as the Holiday Inn Downtown–Mercy Campus), which opened in 1972 at Interstate 235 and Sixth Avenue. The restaurant floor at the top of the twelve-story hotel rotated one full turn per hour, powered by a motor that took about same amount of energy as a sixty-watt lightbulb.

If it weren't for the changing view out the window, you'd never know you were moving, recalled some guests who dined there. Other guests found the experience a bit more disconcerting, especially if they'd had a few drinks and stepped away from their table. Finding their seat again could be a bit confusing.

The idea of enjoying a meal and a cocktail while rotating 360 degrees in a sky-high setting might not sound practical, but when you add a spectacular view to the mix, what's not to like? The remarkable views of Des Moines from the Top O' the Tower were especially striking at night. "That dining room still offers one of the best views of Des Moines," said Bob Conley, owner of Holiday Inn Downtown–Mercy Campus.

Revolving dining rooms were all the rage by the 1960s, not only for their novelty but also as symbols of progress. People got a taste of this with the

The Top O' the Tower restaurant at the Holiday Inn opened in 1972 at Interstate 235 and Sixth Avenue. The restaurant floor at the top of the twelve-story hotel rotated one full turn per hour. *Author's collection.*

revolving floor of the Space Needle's restaurant when it first opened at the 1962 Seattle World's Fair.

Some hotel chains reported that revolving restaurants increased business 50 percent, compared to comparable stationary restaurants. Children sometimes wanted to visit the Holiday Inn to "ride the restaurant."

The Top O' the Tower at the Holiday Inn offered a variety of dining options. The August 18, 1974 issue of the *Des Moines Sunday Register* included an advertisement for The Top O' the Tower Sunday buffet for $3.35 (or $1.75 for children under twelve) from 11:00 a.m. to 4:00 p.m. The menu included roast baron of beef, southern fried chicken, salad bar, hot vegetables, rolls and butter, dessert, coffee, tea and milk.

The Top O' the Tower also became a destination of choice for elegant dinner dates, holiday parties, high school proms and more. "In 1976 or so I made a list of restaurants I wanted to go to on a date or prom," wrote Kimberly Pedersen in a 2016 post on the "Lost Des Moines" Facebook group. The Top O' the Tower made the cut, along with the Rusty Scupper, Colorado Feed & Grain, the Crystal Tree, The Pier, Babe's, Eddie Webster's, the Cork & Cleaver, Felix & Oscars, Riccelli's and others.

When the Top O' the Tower restaurant first opened, singing waiters served the guests. "We used to serenade the tables between waiting on them and then had short stage shows several times a night," noted Mike Spangler, a former singing waiter who shared his memories of the Top O' the Tower on the "Lost Des Moines" Facebook group. The challenge with singing waiters became clear early on, however. "Either a waiter was a good server but couldn't sing, or vice versa. It was hard to find all those skills in one person," Conley said.

Entertainment was part of the ambiance at the Holiday Inn even after the singing waiters were gone. Various people on the "Lost Des Moines" Facebook group recalled the punk rock band the Ramones playing there in 1983, while others remember the male vocal quartet the Four Freshmen and rock-and-roll singer Fabian playing the Top O' the Tower.

The time came, however, for the revolving dining room to make its last spin around the city. The dining room quit revolving around 2017, Conley said, noting that insurance companies and firefighters considered it a hazard. While the Top O' the Tower restaurant is long gone, the space is now a banquet area that continues to offer exceptional views of downtown Des Moines.

There are still revolving restaurants scattered across the globe, including the elegant Top of the World Restaurant located more than eight hundred feet above Las Vegas in the Stratosphere Casino, Hotel & Tower. The next time you're near downtown Des Moines, glance up at the Space Age–looking half-circle projecting from the Holiday Inn Downtown–Mercy Campus and recall an era when the city's revolving restaurant took fine dining to new heights.

CHAPTER 5

A Taste of Elegance at the Younkers Tea Room

Elegance. Grandeur. Sophistication. All defined the iconic Younkers Tea Room, which graced downtown Des Moines for nearly one hundred years. While the Younkers Tea Room closed in 2005, glorious memories of the stunning décor, fine dining and Younkers' famous Rarebit Burgers, chicken salad, spinach salad, sticky rolls and more live on.

"The Tea Room was the most elegant place I'd ever been—like a stateroom from Buckingham Palace magically transported to the Middle West of America," recalled Des Moines native and best-selling author Bill Bryson, whose book *The Life and Times of the Thunderbolt Kid* detailed a visit to the Younkers Tea Room with his mother and sister when he was about eight years old. "Everything about it was starched and classy and calm."

"Classy" also described the Younkers department store, which was founded in Keokuk, Iowa, in 1856 and had been located in downtown Des Moines at Seventh and Walnut Streets since 1899. The Younker brothers who owned the store were always looking for ways to stay at the forefront of retail trends. This began to involve dining trends as well.

In 1890, Harry Selfridge, the visionary manager of the Chicago department store Marshall Field & Company, showed how successful an upscale tea room could be. By 1903, his store's tea room was serving was serving three thousand people per day, noted Vicki Ingram in her 2016 book *Younkers: The Friendly Store.*

Other department store owners quickly realized that encouraging shoppers to dine at their tea rooms reduced the risk that these customers might not

The Younkers department store opened at Seventh Street and Walnut Avenue in downtown Des Moines in 1899. The popular store's famed Tea Room opened its doors in 1913. *Author's collection.*

return if they left the store for lunch. It's likely that Aaron Younker, who had moved to Chicago in 1908 and continued serving as vice-president of Younkers, noted the success of the Marshall Field tea room and encouraged the development of a tea room for Younkers, Ingram said.

News of the plan was greeted with skepticism, however. "When the manager of the Des Moines Club shared with a fellow restaurant owner that Younkers was opening a tea room like the one in Chicago, the two agreed, 'It won't work, no sir, it won't work!'" Ingram wrote.

When the new Younkers Tea Room opened in 1913, however, it quickly became a popular meeting place for bridge clubs, women's groups, banquets and more. By 1949, the *Younker Reporter* newsletter could boast that the Tea Room was held in such high esteem, not only in Des Moines but also throughout Iowa, "that it has become almost as famous as the department store of which it is a part. It is accepted as an institution in the city's life."

Yet the Younkers Tea Room was so much more than that. Its evolution was nothing short of a revolution for women.

TEA ROOMS AND THE EVOLUTION OF THE MODERN WOMAN

While the term *tea room* sometimes conjures up images of high-society, affluent ladies known for their white gloves and extreme propriety, this stereotype is far cry from the vivacity, modernity and stylishness of tea rooms of the early twentieth century. The dawn of the tea room era reflected many women's desires for a more adventurous, independent life.

Prior to the debut of tea rooms, it was quite scandalous in America for a woman to entertain the idea of eating in a restaurant without a man accompanying her. "The restaurant business was closely associated in many people's minds with catering to appetites of all kinds, including sexual appetites," noted Jan Whitaker in her 2002 book *Tea at the Blue Lantern Inn: A Social History of the Tea Room Craze in America.* "For a woman to enter this business at the turn of the [twentieth] century, even as an unescorted patron, was to risk her reputation."

Most women were reluctant to challenge the widespread rule in hotels and fine dining rooms that unescorted women would not be served. Two female travelers in 1906 were embarrassed when the waiter in a New York City restaurant kept badgering them, asking, "When does your escort arrive?" "Escort?" they replied. When they explained they were alone, the headwaiter advised the women that they could not eat there, and they left, "with everyone watching and wondering," Whitaker said.

Crossing the country by car in 1915, etiquette maven Emily Post and a female friend received similar treatment in a hotel they stayed at in Omaha. In the tea room, however, women were never turned away because of their gender.

One of the biggest champions of tea rooms was Alice Foote MacDougall, who owned multiple tea rooms in New York City by the 1920s. She believed that eating should be a fine art. "MacDougall was extremely critical of the mainstream American restaurant, condemning it for being boring, noisy and ugly, and serving mediocre food," Whitaker said. Among her other dislikes were tables set in rows, "greasy gravy" and the "deadly monotony of chain-hotel food."

A tea room, in contrast, created a restful haven from the blare of the street and nourished body and soul. The Younkers Tea Room gave women a public gathering place in the heart of downtown Des Moines where they were welcomed, unlike the men-only clubs, bars and pool halls of the era. It also offered women some freedom from their cooking duties at home.

Oak Room, (Men's Cafe), Hotel Fort Des Moines, Des Moines, Iowa.

There was a time when it was scandalous for a woman to eat in a restaurant without a man accompanying her. This postcard from the Hotel Fort Des Moines noted that the Oak Room was a men's café. *Author's collection.*

By the 1920s and 1930s, establishments like the Younkers Tea Room showed that women no longer had to "subordinate their enjoyment or seek their entertainment solely in the home and the church hall," Whitaker noted.

MEET ME AT YOUNKERS

It's no coincidence that the height of America's tea room craze in the 1920s also intertwined with growth of the American department store. Starting in the nineteenth century, the department store became the first institution to draw women in numbers into the previously all-male city center.

Younkers became *the* place to shop for everything from bedding to clothing to wedding gifts. The Tea Room also became a popular location for wedding receptions, bridal showers, fundraisers and other events. While the Tea Room catered to women of leisure, who often spent their afternoons playing bridge, it also served many workingwomen. These women's ability to afford tea room prices reflected a rising standard of living in urban areas in the postwar 1920s.

Since these patrons had to watch the clock and return to their desks promptly once their lunch break was over, tea rooms concentrated on salads, casseroles and other dishes that could be served quickly. Tea rooms were in the vanguard of culinary change by introducing lighter, well-balanced meals that showcased more vegetables.

The Younkers Tea Room reflected these larger trends, including the rise of the middle class with disposable income and a desire to connect eating to entertainment. Younkers' proximity to the train station and streetcar lines made it easy for patrons from far-flung regions around city and beyond to access this exciting shopping and dining destination in the heart of the city.

Everything about the ornate Younkers Tea Room was designed to capture the imagination. Even the waiting area was elegant, with its spacious lobby and well-appointed sofas and chairs. When Younkers' updated Tea Room and auxiliary dining rooms debuted in late 1925, guests who stepped off the elevator at the fifth floor were ushered into an exotic, Spanish-style *alameda* (public space) and lounge, decorated with Spanish lanterns, hand-woven tapestries, antique Spanish chests bound with iron and chairs with hand-tooled leather seats.

Younkers debuted its updated Tea Room in 1925. Guests who stepped off the elevator at the fifth floor were ushered into an exotic, Spanish-style *alameda* (public space) and lounge. *Author's collection.*

Inside the Tea Room, the professional wait staff were known for being courteous, friendly and attentive. "It almost made you feel like family," recalled one tea room guest. Of the thirty-two waitresses who served in the Tea Room in 1949, nine were twenty-year veterans of the store, while eleven were students who worked evenings, Ingram noted. Attention to detail was evident on every table, which showcased starched white linen tablecloths, cloth napkins, chilled pats of butter and ice water served in crystal goblets.

Tea rooms like the one at Younkers were among the first eating places to showcase salads and transform the bread and rolls served with meals into specialties themselves. The Younkers Tea Room became known for its pastries and sticky rolls. Other Younkers Tea Room favorites included "white meat of chicken salad," homemade salad dressings, clam chowder and burnt almond sponge cake, a fluffy layer cake filled with almond pastry cream, slathered in buttercream frosting and covered in candied almonds.

The Younkers Tea Room became a bastion of delectable dishes, doilies and social graces, accented by glittering chandeliers; soaring, ornate pillars; plush carpeting; potted plants; and sumptuous drapes surrounding large windows that offered spectacular views of the city. It all created an inviting atmosphere reminiscent of a fine home.

This refined domain set the mood for pleasant conversation among friends and family amid the clinking of china dishes and crystal glasses, as soft background music emanated from the grand piano. A young Drake University student named Louis Weertz (better known as Roger Williams) sometimes performed at the Younkers Tea Room, which included a large stage draped with a velvet curtain. Williams, a Des Moines native, became one of America's most popular pianists and was best known for his instrumental rendition of "Autumn Leaves," which became a smash hit in 1955.

Tea rooms weren't just for local patrons. Twentieth-century guidebooks invariably ranked department store tea rooms as good choices for travelers. "Duncan Hines, a restaurant guidebook writer of the 1930s and 1940s, who believed that two-thirds of American eateries were so bad they should be 'padlocked,' often recommended tea rooms as the best places to eat," Whitaker noted. He advised other men that if they would "brave the whimsy," they would discover fine home cooking in tea rooms.

Younkers was included in AAA listings and in Hines's *Adventures in Good Eating*, which described the Tea Room as "nationally known for really good food." In 1962, the Duncan Hines Institute awarded the Younkers Tea Room a silver anniversary service award for having merited inclusion in Hines's book for twenty-five years.

Tea Room Chicken Salad

The Younkers Tea Room was known for a variety of signature dishes, including its chicken salad.

3 cups diced, cooked chicken thighs
1 cup chopped celery
¼ cup chopped onion
¼ cup shelled sunflower seeds
1 cup ranch salad dressing
1 teaspoon celery salt
½ teaspoon dried minced garlic
salt and black pepper (optional)

In a large bowl, combine chicken, celery, onion and sunflower seeds. For dressing, in a small bowl stir together salad dressing, celery salt and garlic. If desired, season to taste with salt and black pepper. Pour dressing over chicken mixture; toss to mix well. Cover and chill for 1 hour. Makes 6 servings.

TEA ROOM CONNECTED IOWANS

While formal attire was not required, people certainly didn't wear jeans and T-shirts to the Younkers Tea Room. For many years, women wore dresses, hats and gloves, along with matching handbags and shoes. "You wanted to give the tea room the respect it deserved," recalled one woman who spoke with Emily Cokeley, who documented the rich history of the Younkers Tea Room in her 1995 thesis at Iowa State University. "You felt important when you went there."

The Younkers Tea Room had a lot to offer customers beyond excellent food at reasonable prices. The Younkers Tea Room Orchestra entertained guests in the 1920s. In the 1930s, Doc Lawson, a well-known local theater organist, brought his nine-piece orchestra to perform in the Tea Room during the lunch hour, as well as dinner dances, Whitaker noted.

During World War II, the Younkers Tea Room featured $1.10 theater dinners, where each patron received a free ticket to the Paramount or Roosevelt Theaters in Des Moines. An illustrated advertisement that appears to hail from this era noted that "Younkers Beautiful Tea Room" served lunch (called "luncheon") from 11:30 a.m. to 2:30 p.m., tea from 2:30 p.m. to 5:00 p.m. and dinner from 5:15 p.m. to 8:00 p.m.

Dining and entertainment went hand in hand at the Younkers Tea Room for generations. Fashion shows held at the Tea Room allowed Younkers to showcase merchandise from its departments. In the 1920s, Younkers' store employees modeled furs and fine jewelry for guests at the Younkers Tea Room.

By the mid-twentieth century, the Younkers Tea Room was providing a unique learning experience for local teenagers who were selected to participate on Younkers' Teen Board. Two students, one boy and one girl, were selected from each Des Moines–area high school based on their leadership qualities, scholastic standing and personal recommendations from school administrators. Part of the Teen Board's duties involved modeling the latest fashions on Saturdays at noon at the Younkers Tea Room.

By the 1970s and 1980s, fashion shows at the Younkers Tea Room also included legendary designers like Roy Halston Frowick, a Des Moines native. At the height of his fame, Halston visited the Younkers Tea Room in the early 1970s for a fashion show featuring his famous ultra-suede shirt-dress. In addition to well-known fashion designers, celebrities also visited the Younkers Tea Room from time to time, including Miss America winners and actress Jane Seymour, who promoted a line of dinnerware she created.

Beyond leisurely meals and fashion shows, the Younkers Tea Room hosted fine arts lectures, book review clubs, private parties and monthly meetings of business leaders and professional organizations, from the Des Moines Women's Club to the Junior League. In the late 1990s and early 2000s, the Tea Room hosted "Let's DU Lunch," a series of lunch-and-learn events sponsored by Drake University for local business professionals.

These events showed that the Younkers Tea Room was never just for the elite or for Des Moines residents. Each March, teenage girls from small towns and farms across Iowa experienced the grandeur and magic of the Younkers Tea Room. Younkers invited everyone playing in the state girls' six-on-six high school basketball tournaments at Veterans' Memorial Auditorium in Des Moines to the Tea Room for a breakfast and style show during their big week in Iowa's capital city.

"I was in awe during my first trip to the Younkers Tea Room," recalled Jan (Pierce) McClue of Lake City, a guard on the Lake City High School

Elegance, grandeur and sophistication defined the iconic Younkers Tea Room. This photo shows a dinner for Younkers' 20-Year Club members in the Tea Room on October 9, 1956. *Courtesy of State Historical Society of Iowa, Des Moines.*

girls' basketball team, which played in the state tournaments in 1965 and 1966. "I grew up on a farm, and my family didn't go out to eat much. The formality of the Tea Room, from the chandeliers to the cloth napkins, made a big impression not only on me, but a lot of my teammates, too."

The *Des Moines Register and Tribune* rented the Tea Room for an annual dinner to honor students who competed in the newspaper's spelling bee. 4-H members were honored at the Tea Room during the Iowa State Fair each summer. Campfire Girls held their annual father-daughter banquet here. The Girl Scouts reserved the Tea Room for a yearly dinner. The Des Moines National Bank took over the space for its Christmas party each year, which required the kitchen staff to cook twenty-four turkeys—one for each table, Ingham noted.

Each year, children flocked to the Tea Room for Easter and Halloween parties. The Tea Room also made a point to appeal to children during meals, serving them from their own china, with menus geared toward children's tastes. The best part came after the meal, when the waitress would bring the "Treasure Chest," from which young guests could choose a gift. While these "gifts" tended to be little more than trinkets wrapped in white tissue paper tied with a pink or blue ribbon, they still generated tremendous excitement. "I was waiting only for the moment when I was invited to step up to the toy box and make a decision," wrote Bill Bryson, who recalled nothing about the food on his first visit to the Tea Room.

When the big moment came, it was tough to make such an important choice. "Every little package looked so perfect and white, so ready to be enjoyed," said Bryson, who eventually chose a midsize package that he dared to shake lightly. Something that sounded like it might be die-cast rattled inside.

Bryson took the package back to his seat and carefully unwrapped the treasure. "It was a miniature doll—an Indian baby in a papoose, beautifully made but patently for a girl. I returned with it and its disturbed packaging to the slightly backward-looking fellow who was in charge of the toy box," Bryson wrote.

When Bryson pointed out that he'd received a doll, the man informed him that was a shame, as kids only got one try at the gift box per visit. "Yes, but it's a *doll*," Bryson insisted. "For a girl."

"'Then you'll just have to git you a little girlfriend to give it to, won'tcha?' he answered and gave me a toothy grin and an unfortunate wink," Bryson recalled.

YOUNKERS OFFERED DINING OPTIONS BEYOND THE TEA ROOM

While the Younkers Tea Room became legendary as a stately, gracious place for lunch or dinner, it wasn't the only dining option at Younkers' downtown store. When Younkers moved the Tea Room to its new west building in 1925, it also opened the Cremona Room in the basement to serve budget meals and snacks. Shoppers, office workers and store employees patronized this luncheonette, which served continuously from 11:00 a.m. to 7:30 p.m., offering affordable lunch and dinner items, including salads, sandwiches and soda fountain treats.

After the Younkers store closed at 5:30 p.m., patrons could enter the Cremona Room directly through the south door on Eighth Street. In the 1940s, the Cremona Room served about 2,500 people daily at lunch and dinner, as well as another 800 at the soda fountain daily, Ingram noted.

REFLECTIONS IN *Younkers* TEA ROOM
DES MOINES, IOWA

Where you meet your friends and enjoy good food

The Younkers Tea Room included glittering chandeliers, ornate pillars, plush carpeting, potted plants and sumptuous drapes surrounding large windows that offered spectacular views of the city. *Author's collection.*

By the 1940s, Younkers also created a third dining option: the Garden Buffet, which offered a wider variety of hot and cold foods than the Tea Room and targeted downtown office workers and other business professionals with an eye on the clock.

Younkers also opened a new bakery on the fifth floor in 1948, separate from the Tea Room operations. The Younkers Bake Shop became famous for its cinnamon rolls, although the bakers also produced rolls, pies, cakes (including angel food cake), biscuits, doughnuts, cookies, eclairs and all sorts of special orders, as well as Younkers' own vanilla ice cream and one special flavor daily. These goodies supplied the Tea Room, Garden Buffet, Cremona Room and a retail counter on the first floor of Younkers' east building.

The 1949 *Younker Reporter* newsletter noted that "a day's volume is approximately 4,000 rolls of various kinds, 30 sheet cakes, 8 to 10 dozen pies, 30 dozen doughnuts, 50 dozen cookies, 3 to 4 gallons of pudding, and 10 or 12 sponge cakes."

Running all these restaurants required a significant investment in the food service industry.

Foodservice manager George Whinery oversaw a small army of cooks, waitresses, dishwashers, laundresses (to wash and iron the cloth napkins and tablecloths), a commissary and other support personnel. In 1949, a relatively small group prepared all the food for the Tea Room and the Garden Room, including a head cook, second cook and three specialists for broiling, frying and vegetables. This all-male crew was supported by an all-female pantry staff who assembled salads, handled coffee and fountain service, dished up desserts and polished silver. Busing the tables and washing and rinsing the china, crystal and silver required a crew of twelve men and women.

As times and tastes changed, Younkers replaced the Cremona Room with a new coffeehouse in 1964. It also replaced the Garden Room with the Rose Room, which catered to office workers on their lunch break and Saturday shoppers by offering moderately priced meals and fountain service.

The Rose Room had its own kitchen, cook and kitchen staff. Formica tabletops and counters paired with light, golden paneling and Mid-century Modern cane-back chairs gave the restaurant a contemporary, informal look. The Rose Room's Syracuse china from New York was described as "one of the outstanding chinas in use in Midwestern dining rooms," Ingham noted.

A large window overlooked the Des Moines skyline to the north. Hand-painted murals on the east and west walls by Dwight Kirsch, former director of the Des Moines Art Center, depicted Iowa-inspired scenes, including a weathered fence, wild roses (Iowa's state flower) and mail boxes with farm buildings in the distance. The Rose Room closed by early 1974, when the Tea Room was enlarged and remodeled.

Parts of the former Rose Room space became a new bakery, while the rest was turned into the Sweet Shoppe, a "gourmet's glee and dieter's downfall," noted the *Younkers Reporter*. Decorated in Colonial style, which was becoming popular due to America's bicentennial in 1976, the little shop served pastries, ice cream, finger sandwiches and freshly ground coffee between 11:00 a.m. and 3:30 p.m.

Foodservice options at Younkers continued in one form or another for many more years, both at the downtown store and other Younkers stores that had opened around Des Moines and the Midwest. The Meadowlark restaurant opened at the Younkers store at the new Merle Hay Mall in Des Moines in 1959, while the Younkers store at the Southridge Mall in Des Moines opened the Peacock Room in 1975. These restaurants were smaller than the restaurants at the downtown Younkers but offered convenient options for hungry shoppers.

In 1980, the Merle Hay Mall store introduced an alternative to fast food with 22 Carats, a sleek, contemporary restaurant offering a health-conscious menu. The restaurant operated under the direction of Michael LaValle, who became one of Des Moines's best-known culinary entrepreneurs and general manager/executive chef at the Embassy Club in Des Moines.

While Younkers' dining options included new entrées, customers of the Tea Room also loved the classics, like Rarebit Burgers (hamburgers with cheese sauce poured on top). These can still be found at various central Iowa restaurants like the Ankeny Diner, whose rarebit burger features spicy cheddar cheese sauce, served open-faced.

Younkers Rarebit Burgers

To make Younkers popular rarebit burgers, cook 8 hamburger patties to 160 degrees Fahrenheit until no pink remains. Place each burger in a toasted hamburger bun. Spoon about ¼ cup of rarebit sauce over each bun. Serve immediately.

Tea Room Rarebit Sauce
⅓ cup cooking oil
⅓ cup flour
1 teaspoon paprika
¼ teaspoon salt
¼ teaspoon dry mustard
2 cups whole milk
1 teaspoon Worcestershire sauce
¼ teaspoon bottled hot pepper sauce
1 cup shredded processed sharp American cheese (4 ounces)

Place oil in a medium saucepan. Stir together flour, paprika, salt and dry mustard. Add flour mixture to oil; cook and stir for 1 minute. Stir in milk all at once. Cook and stir over medium heat until thickened and bubbly. Cook and stir 1 minute more. Remove from heat; stir in Worcestershire sauce and hot pepper sauce. Add cheese and stir until melted. Makes 2 cups.

THE END OF AN ERA: A LEGACY THAT ENDURES

There have been so many memorable aspects of Younkers for Iowans through the years, from delicious dining options to back-to-school shopping. Few events could compare with the festive holiday season at Younkers. Many people remember the spectacular Christmas tree, lavish holiday window decorations and "Breakfast with Santa" that were all part of the downtown Des Moines Younkers experience each December. After families completed their Christmas shopping at Younkers, they often stopped by the Tea Room for lunch. During the holidays, guests could often sample a wide array of treats from an impressive dessert table.

Although Younkers remained a popular shopping destination for Iowa families for decades, the beginning of the end for the downtown Younkers department store and the famed Tea Room started with the rise of the shopping mall era. While many customers remained loyal to the downtown Younkers store, the opening of Merle Hay Mall in Des Moines in 1959, followed by Valley West Mall in West Des Moines in 1975, reduced traffic at the downtown Younkers location. The malls were closer to the Des Moines metro's growing suburbs and offered more convenience.

By then, the Younkers Tea Room had already far outlasted many of its early twentieth-century contemporaries. After World War II ended, for example, most tea rooms, apart from those in department stores, had ceased to thrive and were considered the "old lady of the restaurant industry," according to Jan Whitaker, the author who has documented a social history of the tea room in America.

By the late 1980s and 1990s, the Younkers Tea Room had become one of the last of these elegant relics in the United States. The heyday of downtown shopping had waned, casual Fridays were changing the workplace and many people weren't interested in dressing up just for a meal.

While Younkers remained a flagship brand in Iowa, the business had begun to erode by the 2000s, as discount stores like Walmart continued to gain momentum. Changes in the corporate structure of Younkers, which had been bought out by Saks Inc., also led to the demise of the Younkers Tea Room, which closed permanently in August 2005.

While there was hope for a revival when developers purchased the former Younkers building in 2012 and began renovating the property, those dreams went up in flames on March 29, 2014, when a catastrophic fire ravaged the building.

After the 2014 fire, many feared that it was gone forever. However, the historic Wilkins Building and Tea Room were saved and rehabilitated by Blackbird, a Des Moines–based real estate developer. Since reopening in 2017, the Tea Room has provided a unique venue for weddings and wedding receptions, corporate conferences, cocktail parties, fundraisers and other events.

Younkers itself didn't survive changing times, however. Various mergers and acquisitions pushed remaining Younkers stores into the Bon-Ton chain. After Bon-Ton filed for bankruptcy, the company's 256 stores, including 49 Younkers stores, had closed by the end of August 2018.

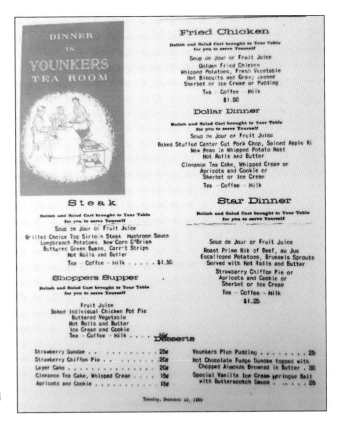

Dining options from this Younkers Tea Room menu, dated December 22, 1959, included the soup de jour, chicken pot pie, strawberry chiffon pie, cinnamon tea cake and more. *Author's collection.*

Yet the legacy of Younkers and its beloved Tea Room live on. The long-term effects of the tea room craze that fueled the rise of the Younkers Tea Room more than a century ago are still felt today, in ways few people suspect.

"Tea rooms introduced candles and flowers to restaurant tables," Whitaker noted. "Tea rooms restyled restaurant interiors, cultivating atmosphere. They hired college girls as waitresses and substituted friendly hostesses for stiffly tuxedoed maître d's. They demonstrated that women could succeed in the restaurant industry and that money could be made in the food business, even without alcohol. They showed that women were a solid customer base and that families with children could be accommodated."

The Younkers Tea Room, like other tea rooms across America, also succeeded in changing the entire landscape for female diners. As the article "The Top-Secret Feminist History of Tea Room" (accessible via JSTOR.org) noted, "We have these establishments to thank for a world where women can dine out comfortably on their own."

Chapter 6

Cooking Up Change

Restaurants, Race Relations and Civil Rights

If you white, you all right.
If you brown, stick around.
If you black, git back, git back, git back.

Those lyrics came from a song written in 1948 by Big Bill Broonzy, an African American blues singer, songwriter and guitarist who spent time in central Iowa in 1950. While Iowa has a rich history of African American culture, the story is also complicated by racism. This had become painfully clear by the mid-twentieth century when a young Black mother named Edna Griffin was refused service at a soda fountain in downtown Des Moines and achieved a major victory for civil rights in America. So, how did this happen? Let's take a look back in time to gain some insight into the complex realm of civil rights in Iowa.

In many ways, Iowa was a leader in civil rights. In 1839, the Iowa Territorial Supreme Court ruled that a slave named Ralph Montgomery could not be extradited to Missouri after he failed to raise the $550 he promised to pay to buy his freedom. In honor of the 170th anniversary of the landmark court ruling, the sculpture *Shattering Silence* was installed near the Iowa Supreme Court building on the top of the hill overlooking the Des Moines skyline. The iconic artwork honors those moments when Iowa has been at the forefront of breaking the silence of inequality and commemorates Iowans who refused to stand by silently when they saw injustice.

In the volatile years before the Civil War, a number of Iowans took great risks to help fugitive slaves escape to freedom via the Underground Railroad, which ran across the southern third of the state in the 1850s. Iowans from Tabor and Lewis in southwest Iowa to Winterset and Grinnell in central Iowa and on into Salem and other communities in eastern Iowa helped slaves on their perilous journey, potentially risking their own safety in the process.

George Washington Carver, a man who had been born into slavery in Missouri, found opportunity in Iowa. He earned his bachelor's degree in 1894 from Iowa State College in Ames, where he also earned his master's degree in 1896. His skills in plant breeding helped him become the school's first African American graduate and faculty member.

By World War I, Des Moines was helping shatter racial boundaries in the military. In May 1917, the federal government announced the creation of a training camp for 1,200 Black officers at Fort Des Moines. The local white community was, for the most part, receptive toward the 1,250 candidates. By October 1917, Fort Des Moines had graduated 639 men, including captains, first lieutenants and second lieutenants.

With success stories like this, it's tempting to think that racism didn't exist in Iowa, yet it did. "They talk about segregation in the South," noted Ruby Haddix, who grew up in northern Iowa and is quoted at the African American Museum of Iowa in Cedar Rapids. "It was just as bad in the North, only they were real subtle about it."

Des Moines wasn't immune from this subtle racism, although the capital city did have the largest number of Black-owned businesses in Iowa, according to the book *Outside In: African-American History in Iowa, 1838–2000*. It also included the thriving Center Street neighborhood, which was located northwest of downtown Des Moines and home to much of the city's Black population.

The neighborhood grew during World War I when Black officers were allowed to train at Fort Des Moines. As the Center Street neighborhood flourished, it became the hub of the African American community of Des Moines from the 1920s until the 1960s.

The area's business district included restaurants, barbershops, nightclubs, grocery stores, pharmacies, law offices, pool halls, hotels, laundries, a funeral home, service stations, a movie theater, a photography studio, a beauty school and a print shop. Many neighborhood businesses attracted customers by advertising in the *Iowa Bystander*, the city's Black newspaper.

While Center Street was a thriving community by day, it truly came alive at night. Not only were the bars and clubs filled with music and people, but the streets were always lively in this unique district that hosted some of the biggest names in entertainment in the 1930s, '40s, and '50s.

Families would drive to Center Street, park their car and sit on the hood to watch all the activity. Food vendors would wander the streets all night, selling tamales and more to families and inebriated club goers, noted Drake University student and saxophonist Roland Hart, who published "The Music of Center Street: Des Moines' Lost Jazz Hub" in the Greater Des Moines Community Jazz Center's spring 2013 newsletter.

One of Center Street's first performance venues, Theater Lincoln, located at Twelfth and Center, hosted shows produced by African Americans. Theater Lincoln shared a building with a restaurant (the Garden Café) and the Shelburn Gardens. The Shelburn would later be known as the Billiken Ballroom, which hosted its first show on September 19, 1938.

While bouncers at the other ballrooms in town would often refuse to let African Americans in, even when the performers were Black, the Billiken never turned them away. The Billiken hosted some of the most popular entertainers of the era. "Center Street was not just an area of town but a world within a world," added Honesty Parker in her 2011 book *African Americans of Des Moines and Polk County.* "When big bands came to town, these nationally-known celebrities played at white hotels and clubs but stayed on Center Street. The likes of Duke Ellington, Louie Armstrong, Ella Fitzgerald and various others spent many nights on Center Street."

The Sepia Supper Club became another notable Center Street club. The Sepia was not only a jazz club but also home to the local chapter of the National Association for the Advancement of Colored People (NAACP), the Black Musicians Union and a restaurant, Hart noted. The Sepia featured Saturday night shrimp dinners at the restaurant.

Along with good food, the Center Street clubs like the Billiken and Sepia were key clubs in the 1940s and 1950s. While clubs were not allowed to serve beer and liquor after 2:00 a.m., patrons could store their own hard liquor in a locked box at the venue, accessible only by the bartender and the patron. "This made the clubs especially attractive to after-hours musicians and facilitated late night jam sessions, as the clubs were open 24 hours," Hart said. "Center Street never shut down, giving Des Moines the reputation of being the 'Sin City of the Prairie.'"

RESTAURANTS LEFT A BAD TASTE IN GABRIEL COOLS'S MOUTH

Since Black members of the community were welcome at few white eating establishments, a variety of restaurants thrived in the Center Street neighborhood, noted *Outside In*. When a man named Gabriel Cools visited Des Moines in 1918, he indicated that there were twelve restaurants, but only two were "in any true sense restaurants," he wrote. "The others are more or less unpretentious places which cater to the less discriminating classes."

Cools went on to offer a description of a typical restaurant: "The café was in the basement. There were half a dozen tables over which were thrown pieces of brown paper which functioned as table cloths, and these were not clean. The concrete floor was unclean…with no sign of having been washed in a decade. And to add to the grotesqueness of the place, a new Victrola was being displayed with conspicuous position."

Two other establishments received slightly better reviews. "One sees…an attempt at conforming to some kind of hygienic standards," Cools wrote. "They were kept fairly clean and the service at least was not repulsive. The proprietor of the smaller place was more attentive to the conduct of the business. Everything was new, from the soda water fountain to the chairs, and the tables were covered with clean white cloths—a decided improvement over the brown paper covers."

SOUL FOOD, DES MOINES STYLE

One of the most popular Center Street restaurants was the eighteen-seat Community Luncheonette, which opened in 1935. Operated by husband-and-wife team Arthur P. and Goletha Trotter, the Community Luncheonette opened early for breakfast and stayed open until late at night. "During World War II, when the Black population of Des Moines grew significantly, the Trotters served three hundred meals daily," noted *Outside In*. "They also cooked for visiting black celebrities."

The Community Luncheonette lasted until 1956, when the Trotters retired. Then the restaurant became the Burke Café, operated by R.J. Burke. Today, the Burke Café is only a memory, much like the Center Street neighborhood itself, which disappeared in the wake of urban renewal in this area, including the development of Interstate 235 and the construction of new housing projects in the 1960s.

Business cards for Sampson's Chicken Shack, which were printed in Des Moines's Center Street neighborhood, noted, "If you are in the dog house at home, you're always welcome at Sampson's Chicken Shack." *Author's collection.*

In years past, the African American neighborhood on Des Moines's east side was home to a restaurant and night spot called Sampson's Chicken Shack. George and Elizabeth Sampson's place was located in a house that had been converted into a restaurant, with a dance area in an annex. The Sampsons' menu was simple, with only eight entrées that included chicken, fish, steak and barbecued rib dinners. They also hosted live bands at their restaurant, which was located at 1246 East Seventeenth Street.

Advertising cards printed in Des Moines's Center Street neighborhood by Robert Patten told prospective customers, "If you are in the dog house at home, you're always welcome at Sampson's Chicken Shack."

In later years, African Americans would continue to serve up distinct flavors of Des Moines. Big Daddy's BBQ cultivated a reputation as the best barbecue pit in town. NBC News anchor Tom Brokaw would request that his driver pick up an order of ribs there when he was in Des Moines, noted the *Des Moines Register.* A Capitol Park neighborhood favorite, Big Daddy's BBQ closed in 2018.

Patton's Restaurant at 1552 East Grand Avenue began offering southern-inspired fare in 2011. Along with a weekly soul food buffet, owner and cook Pam Patton, a former diversity consultant at Des Moines–based Principal Financial, served up fried chicken, greens and peas, sweet tea and sweet potato pie until the restaurant closed in February 2017.

THE ROCKET ROOM RAN ADS FOR "COLORED BOYS"

While Des Moines has offered diverse dining establishments through the years, diversity meant different things to different generations. Consider the Rocket Room at the Hotel Savery.

The Rocket Room operated in downtown Des Moines for more than thirty years. An ad in the May 6, 1941 edition of the *Des Moines Tribune* highlighted how the "air cooled" Rocket Room offered fried chicken, cooked to order, "the American way, with livers and giblets," along with longbranch (fried) potatoes, spring salad, bread-and-butter sandwiches and "that good Rocket Room" coffee for sixty-five cents.

By late 1946, the Hotel Savery had reopened the revamped Rocket Room coffee shop and dining room. The property had been without a dining room and kitchen since the Savery Hotel was remodeled to house the Women's Auxiliary Corps during World War II. The new Rocket Room seated 150 people and was open seven days a week from 7:00 a.m. to 1:00 a.m.

The Rocket Room assured that "a warm welcome awaits all," yet the wording of the restaurant's classified ads from this era indicates that skin color mattered. Consider the September 19, 1948 edition of the *Des Moines Register*, which included want ads for busboys at a number of downtown hotels, including the Hotel Fort Des Moines, the Hotel Franklin and the Hotel Savery's Rocket Room. Only the Rocket Room ad singled out Black people, specifying that "bus boys—colored—apply with Mrs. Tibbetts." Subsequent newspaper want ads for the Rocket Room, which billed itself

The Rocket Room coffee shop and dining room at the Hotel Savery in downtown Des Moines advertised in local newspapers for "colored bus boys" in the late 1940s and early 1950s. *Author's collection.*

as "Iowa's finest coffee shop," continued to specify "bus boy—colored" into the early 1950s.

By 1959, classified ads seeking waitresses for the Rocket Room in a "first-class hotel coffee shop" noted that meals and uniforms were furnished, plus paid vacation, insurance and other benefits were offered, along with "excellent earnings." While applicants were encouraged to apply with Mrs. Wilber, there's no indication whether the Rocket Room was looking for "colored" busboys.

EDNA GRIFFIN: HOW FOOD HELPED FUEL THE CIVIL RIGHTS MOVEMENT

It would take an incident at a downtown drugstore soda fountain to propel civil rights issues to the forefront in Des Moines and forever change how Iowa would live up to its democratic ideals.

It all started on a hot afternoon on July 7, 1948. Des Moines resident Edna Griffin, thirty-nine, stopped by Katz Drug Store at Seventh and Locust Streets with her infant daughter, Phyllis, and two friends, John Bibbs, twenty-two, and Leonard Hudson, thirty-two. All were African American.

While Hudson went to look for some batteries, Griffin and Bibbs took seats at the lunch counter. Some accounts say they ordered ice cream sundaes, while others say ice cream sodas. In any case, as the waitress walked toward the ice cream dispenser to serve them, a young white man came by and whispered in her ear.

The waitress then informed Griffin and Bibbs that she was not allowed to serve them because of their race. By that time, Hudson had rejoined his companions. The three adults asked to see the waitress's supervisor, and she obliged, summoning the soda fountain manager, C.L. Gore, twenty-two, who had come north from Florida just two years earlier. "The tenor of that exchange would later be disputed," noted Noah Lawrence in his article "Since It Is My Right, I Would Like to Have It: Edna Griffin and the Katz Drug Store Desegregation Movement," published in the *Annals of Iowa* in the fall of 2008.

Griffin, Bibbs and Hudson said the conversation was hushed and polite; Gore claimed the three Black patrons caused a disturbance. In any case, Griffin, Bibbs and Hudson didn't get any ice cream that day, despite appealing to store manager Maurice Katz. More significantly, Griffin decided to use

Left: Within eighteen months of being refused service at Katz Drug Store in 1948, Edna Griffin had launched successful civil and criminal lawsuits against store owner Maurice Katz. During the trials, Griffin's service in the Women's Army Corps (WAC) was noted. *Courtesy of Stanley Griffin Jr.*

Below: Katz Drug Store was located at Seventh and Locust Streets in Des Moines. The chain, which was notorious for refusing to serve African Americans, agreed to cease all discriminatory policies by December 1949. *Courtesy of Stanley Griffin Jr.*

the incident as the impetus to topple the segregationist policies of the Katz Drug Store chain.

Founded in 1914 in Kansas City, Missouri, the Katz Drug Store chain became more than a place to pick up prescriptions in cities across the Midwest. "A trip to your neighborhood Katz store meant enjoying a burger and shake at the soda fountain with your sweetheart, or going with your dad on a Saturday morning to get candy or a comic book for you and fishing tackle for him," stated a nostalgic look at "The Enduring Legacy of Katz Drug Stores," which ran in a 2014 issue of Kansas City's *435 Magazine*.

During its fifty-seven-year run, Katz was known for discounted pricing, salespeople in every department, its variety of merchandise and extensive promotions. It grew to include sixty-five stores in five states, including the store in downtown Des Moines.

Within eighteen months of being refused service at Katz that summer day in 1948, Griffin had mobilized citizens to take action against the chain, launched successful civil and criminal lawsuits against store owner Maurice Katz and earned vindication when the Katz Drug Store capitulated to demands by agreeing to cease all discriminatory policies by December 1949.

The Katz lawsuits would affect restaurants across Des Moines and Iowa, all because of one brave lady who refused to be silenced.

The Beginnings of a Grass-Roots Activist

Edna (Williams) Griffin was born in 1909 in Kentucky. When she was an infant, her family moved to a farm near Walpole, New Hampshire. Raised with Unitarian/Quaker faith traditions, Griffin attended junior high school in New Hampshire, graduated two years early from high school in Massachusetts in 1928 and attended Fisk University in Nashville, Tennessee. Attending a historically Black university was a new experience for Griffin, as she had lived in a predominantly white farming community up to that point.

At Fisk, Griffin met her future husband, Dr. Stanley Griffin. She cleaned houses to pay her tuition, took classes and earned her bachelor's degree in sociology in 1933. By some accounts, Griffin believed that Fisk was too conservative. As a young woman, she started taking much more active role as a peaceful protestor. Griffin was arrested for joining striking teachers on a picket line, plus she marched against Mussolini's invasion of Ethiopia.

After college, Stanley and Edna Griffin lived in New York City, Georgia, Tennessee and Massachusetts before moving to Des Moines on January

2, 1947, so Stanley could attend the Still Osteopathic School of Medicine (known today as Des Moines University).

Edna gave birth to the first of the couple's three children, Phyllis, in 1947. Despite being a new mother, Edna became an activist in Des Moines almost immediately. Within the next year, she had already been appointed to leadership posts as chair of the organizing committee of the Progressive Party for Iowa's Fifth Congressional District and secretary-treasurer of the Des Moines branch of the Communist Party, noted the *Annals of Iowa*.

Griffin benefited from her husband's work as a doctor who made house calls to many African American and Mexican American members of the community. These connections helped widen her network of potential activists. Griffin also continued to expand her knowledge by enrolling as a graduate student at Drake University in Des Moines.

"Although she was only 5'2" and 125 pounds in 1949, this petite woman would be a thorn in the side of Maurice Katz and many others who wished to maintain the status quo," the according to the *Annals of Iowa*.

Why Won't They Enforce the Laws?

The Katz Drug Store chain had maintained a policy of de facto segregation for decades by refusing to serve Black patrons, despite Iowa's state law that expressly forbade discrimination in public accommodations, including lunch counters.

Several different individuals and organizations had failed in bringing charges against Katz before Griffin ultimately succeeded. Issues of the *Iowa Bystander*, a newspaper published in Des Moines since 1894 and geared toward an African American audience, detailed an eighteen-year battle to end segregation at Katz. Criminal prosecutions were brought against the drugstore in 1943, 1944 and 1947, but owner Maurice Katz was acquitted in all three cases. In addition, at least fourteen civil cases brought against Katz had failed.

A letter to the national offices of the NAACP offered a snapshot of race relations in Des Moines in the mid-1940s. In 1944, V.V. Oak, the editor of the *Negro College Quarterly*, evaluated Des Moines as "not a badly prejudiced city," but one where "there have been many incidents…which have proven very annoying."

Oak then described an episode in which a "colored lady" had been denied service at "one of the main Katz's drug stores." The woman had filed a lawsuit against the store, which so angered Katz's management that it ordered "all the drugstores to refuse certain services to all Negroes, civilian and military." That included African American women training in the Women's Army Corps (WAC) at Fort Des Moines during World War II. Oak lamented that when the woman later dropped her case, the manager "took this as evidence of a lack of solidarity in the Negro race."

While Katz's discriminatory practices were notorious, the NAACP's internal documents show that the organization could find few Black citizens willing to prosecute or testify against the company. Griffin was acutely aware of this after she moved to Des Moines, according to the *Annals of Iowa*.

Iowa and much of America were largely segregated in the late 1940s. It wasn't until 1947 that Jackie Robinson of the Brooklyn Dodgers became the first Black player in modern Major League Baseball. Back in Des Moines, a 1948 editorial in the *Iowa Bystander* described two ways Iowa's capital city failed to meet the standard of a democratic city: the systematic effort to ban Black citizens from skilled trades and the fact that "eating accommodations downtown are miserable and every effort to change them are met with stern opposition of the small as [well as] the large establishments."

Iowa's first civil rights law, passed in 1884, had outlawed discrimination in "inns, public conveyances, barbershops, theaters, and other places of public amusement." The law was amended in 1892 to include "restaurants, chophouses, lunch counters and all other places where refreshments are served," yet it contained no practical enforcement mechanism.

Thanks to a concerted effort by the Des Moines branch of the NAACP, the law was again amended in 1923 so that violations could be heard by a local magistrate rather than a grand jury. This still didn't solve the problems of de facto segregation, however. It was tough to convince Iowa's citizens, including state prosecutors, that denying civil rights to Black citizens was a significant enough problem to merit action. Black citizens made up just a fraction of Iowa's population, and many Iowans had rarely seen a Black person, let alone refused one a job or a meal at a restaurant.

Taking Katz to Trial

Then along came Griffin. She was a vocal community leader, a rarity for a woman at the time. She was also a civil rights warrior who knew her battleground. "She wasn't afraid to stand up for unpopular causes," noted her son Stanley Griffin Jr. "Mother was considered a little too radical, though, for many people at the time, even the black community."

Some people wondered if Griffin and her friends deliberately targeted Katz Drug Store to make a point. Phyllis Griffin, who was quoted in the *Annals of Iowa*, believed that her mother probably was aware of Katz's history of discrimination.

Years later, when Edna Griffin was asked to share details about that July day when she was refused service at Katz, she told a *Des Moines Register* reporter, "It was as if you were suddenly not a citizen, not a member of the community."

Griffin would not give up. After being refused service, she began consulting with fellow members of the Progressive Party and lawyers for the NAACP to develop a legal strategy. First, bring a criminal case against Katz due to noncompliance, then proceed with civil suits. While Griffin wasn't afraid to take bold steps to help end segregation in Des Moines, she had to maintain a difficult balance, according to the *Annals of Iowa*. That meant challenging the law while operating within its confines and taking part in social activism without appearing to be a radical activist.

Action against Katz moved quickly after Griffin and her friends were denied service on July 7, 1948. By July 10, Griffin, Bibbs and Hudson had filed charges against Katz in Des Moines Municipal Court. Two days later, Maurice Katz pleaded not guilty and was released on bond. A trial was held on October 6, 1948.

During the trial, Bibbs recalled that C.L. Gore, the soda fountain manager, explained that he could not serve Bibbs and Griffin because "it is the policy of our store that we don't serve colored; we don't have the equipment." Bibbs claimed that he and Griffin then asked to speak to Mr. Katz, the store manager, who told them, "I cater to a large volume of white trade and don't have the proper equipment to serve you."

Bibbs insisted the entire incident was orderly and polite. Leonard Hudson corroborated Bibb's testimony. The only feasible defense for Katz would be that denial of service was justified not because Bibbs, Griffin and Hudson were African American but because they were causing a disturbance.

When it was C.L. Gore's turn to testify, he recalled being alerted to the presence of Bibbs, Griffin and Hudson when his "attention was first attracted by loud voices." Gore said that he went to inquire what the problem was, and his recollection of the three was that "they were demanding service, and they were very rude."

Maurice Katz's testimony was consistent with Gore's. According to Katz, "He [Bibbs] said, 'We are members of the Progressive Party, and we are going to make a test case out of this.' I said, 'A test case out of what?' And

The African American Museum of Iowa in Cedar Rapids includes a replica of the Katz Drug Store lunch counter in Des Moines where Edna Griffin led grass-roots efforts to secure civil rights for African Americans. *Author's collection.*

then Mrs. Griffin spoke up and said, 'You know what we are talking about. Don't act dumb.'"

During cross-examination, when Assistant County Attorney Paul McDonnell asked Gore, "Have you ever served colored people in Katz Drug Store?" the young fountain manager admitted he had not. Later, when Katz was asked the same question, he stated, "I haven't served any."

After four hours of deliberation, a jury of six white women rendered their verdict on October 7, 1948. They determined that Maurice Katz and C.L. Gore were guilty of denying service to the African American patrons. Katz was fined $50 (nearly $500 in today's dollars). This became the first legal setback the Katz Drug Store chain faced. It also marked a major victory not only for Griffin, Bibbs and Hudson but also for the entire African American community in Des Moines.

Yet the fight was far from over.

Griffin Led Protests, Sit-Ins and Boycotts

Katz appealed his case to the Iowa Supreme Court. It would be a year before the court heard the case. In the meantime, the battles between the drugstore and the civil rights advocates raged on.

Griffin kept the pressure on Katz by filing a civil case with a $10,000 damage suit against the company. Her lawyer, Charles P. Howard, was one of Iowa's most prominent Black attorneys. Howard had graduated from the Fort Des Moines Army Officer Candidate School in 1917, served as a second lieutenant with the 92nd Division, 366th Infantry, in France during World War I and later returned to Des Moines, where he graduated from Drake University's law school in 1922. He called Griffin's case "the most important lawsuit I've ever tried," according to the *Annals of Iowa*.

During the trial, which began on October 10, 1949, Griffin emphasized her service in the Women's Army Corps during World War II, as well as her role as a mother, to establish her respectability. Howard also emphasized Griffin's educational background and her role as the wife of a Des Moines doctor and college professor.

On October 15, 1949, the all-white jury decided the case in Griffin's favor, although they chose to award her only one dollar in damages. Still, Griffin and her lawyers considered the verdict a moral victory.

Despite losing both the criminal and civil cases, the Katz Drug Store still refused to serve African Americans. Shortly after her civil trial ended, Griffin formed the Committee-to-End-Jim-Crow-at-Katz-Drugstore. The committee was open to "every Negro and white person who believes in civil rights as a safeguard to democracy."

Although the committee did not form officially until after Griffin's civil case ended, Griffin had helped coordinate a series of protests, sit-ins and boycotts in 1948 and 1949 to impede Katz's ability to run his business successfully. In fact, she initiated the initial pickets against Katz within ten days of the July 7, 1948 incident at Katz's soda fountain that started everything.

Griffin planned the first protest for Saturday, July 17, 1948. Volunteers of various races, religious faiths and political views joined the committee. "If you interact with a diverse group of people who are different from you, it will make you stronger," noted Griffin's son Stanley, a 1969 graduate of Roosevelt High School in Des Moines who now lives in Atlanta, Georgia.

Volunteers met on Saturdays at the Katz Drug Store from 11:00 a.m. to 2:00 p.m., the store's busiest time of day. They sent waves of members to take turns sitting in at Katz's lunch counter, while other members remained

Edna Griffin (*second from left*) led pickets and sit-ins at Katz Drug Store in Des Moines, years before famed lunch counter sit-ins would capture national attention in Greensboro, North Carolina, in 1960. *Courtesy of Stanley Griffin Jr.*

outside on the sidewalk handing out pamphlets stating "Katz is More Powerful than Iowa" and carrying placards with messages like "Counter Service for Whites Only, This is Hitler's Old Baloney, Don't Buy at Katz."

The sit-ins at Katz in Des Moines foreshadowed the famous Greensboro civil rights protest of 1960, when young African American students staged a sit-in at a segregated Woolworth's lunch counter in Greensboro, North Carolina, and refused to leave after being denied service. That sit-in movement soon spread to college towns throughout the South.

The Committee-to-End-Jim-Crow-at-Katz-Drugstore in Des Moines also helped people who were denied service by Katz employees to file additional lawsuits against the company to keep the pressure on. Griffin herself filed a second lawsuit against Katz on November 12, 1949, demanding that the district court revoke Katz's restaurant and cigarette licenses and declare the company a chronic law violator. Four other members of the organization brought suits against Katz the same day, noted the *Annals of Iowa*.

The pressure on Katz was mounting. Court battles were piling up, and protestors were growing emboldened. On December 2, 1949, Katz settled out of court, agreeing to pay $1,000 and end the store's discriminatory practices. The *Iowa Bystander* reported that "Negro patrons entered the store on December 3 and began receiving courteous service at the Katz Drug store luncheonette."

The battle had been won.

Setting the Stage for the Civil Rights Era

Griffin's victory against Katz Drug Store was one of many localized civil rights struggles nationwide in the post–World War II era that coalesced into the great civil rights mobilization of the 1950s and 1960s. "The success of the civil rights movement owes a great deal to the efforts of older activists such as Griffin, who worked in obscurity throughout the 1940s and 1950s," noted the *Annals of Iowa*.

After her successful role in the Katz struggle, Griffin remained in Des Moines for the rest of her life and continued her activism, working with organized labor unions, farmers and others. "Mother was so much more than the Katz Drug Store incident," said her son Stanley. "She was never interested in stopping her fight for equality, because she saw how much work needed to be done."

Griffin has been described as "Iowa's Rosa Parks" for her leadership, although she took a stand seven years before Parks refused to surrender her seat to a white passenger on a segregated bus in Montgomery, Alabama, in 1955.

There was always a fire in Griffin's eyes and an intensity behind her calm demeanor, according to people who knew her. As civil rights issues gained national attention, Griffin founded Des Moines's chapter of the Congress of Racial Equality (CORE) in 1963. That same year, she organized a group of Iowans to travel to the March on Washington, where they heard Dr. Martin Luther King Jr. deliver his famous "I Have a Dream" speech in August 1963 at the Lincoln Memorial. This speech was one of the many efforts that helped bring about landmark federal legislation, including the Civil Rights Act of 1964 and Voting Rights Act of 1965.

Griffin was inducted into the Iowa Women's Hall of Fame in 1985 and the Iowa African Americans' Hall of Fame in 1998. Fifty years after she and her friends were refused service at the soda fountain at Katz Drug Store in the Flynn Building, leaders from across Iowa gathered there at the intersection of Seventh and Locust in Des Moines on July 7, 1998, to honor Griffin, John Bibbs and Leonard Hudson for the courage they'd shown by forcing the city to live up to its ideals. A plaque was installed to commemorate their civil rights victory. The building that housed Katz Drug Store all those years ago was renamed and is now known as the Edna Griffin Building. This adaptive reuse project is now home to residential apartment units, many of which qualify as affordable housing.

Right: After her successful role in the Katz Drug Store case, Griffin remained in Des Moines for the rest of her life and continued her activism, working with organized labor unions, farmers and others. "Mother was so much more than the Katz Drug Store incident," said her son, Stanley. "She was never interested in stopping her fight for equality, because she saw how much work needed to be done." *Courtesy of Stanley Griffin Jr.*

Below: In 2004, Edna Griffin's three children, elected officials, local elementary school children and representatives of the Iowa Department of Transportation inaugurated the Edna M. Griffin Bridge in Des Moines. *Courtesy of Stanley Griffin Jr.*

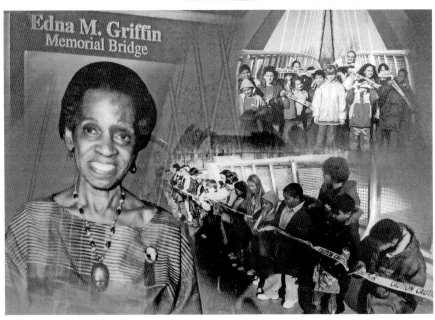

In October 2019, the Des Moines–based convenience store chain Kum & Go announced plans to open a three-thousand-square-foot store in the Edna Griffin Building. The new concept is part of a nationwide trend of traditional convenience and grocery stores opening urban retail locations that focus on healthier items.

Griffin's legacy lives on in other downtown Des Moines locations as well. A few years after Griffin passed away in 2000, several of Iowa's top lawmakers, including Lieutenant Governor Sally Pederson and U.S. Representative Leonard Boswell, gathered on May 10, 2004, with Griffin's three children, a group of elementary school children and representatives of the Iowa Department of Transportation (DOT) to inaugurate the Edna M. Griffin Bridge, a blue footbridge located near East Sixth Street that allows people to safely cross Interstate 235.

Jenny Schiltz's fourth-grade class at Longfellow Elementary School in Des Moines won the honor of opening the bridge. Their suggestion to call this the Edna M. Griffin Memorial Bridge was chosen as the winning entry in the pedestrian bridge-naming contest sponsored by the Iowa DOT.

"A bridge is an apt metaphor for Edna Griffin, a woman whose action helped put to rest the segregationist policies of Katz Drug Company, and who, in doing so, helped usher in a new era of civil rights activism marked by mass mobilization and a firm commitment to nonviolent direct action," noted the *Annals of Iowa*.

CHAPTER 7

Diners, Drive-Ons, Food and Fun

Sometimes what's old is new again. Consider how urban planners seeking to revitalize neighborhoods are focusing on the critical role that "third places" can play in strengthening our sense of community. "Third places" is a modern term coined by Ray Oldenburg, a professor emeritus of sociology at the University of West Florida in Pensacola. It refers to places where people spend time between home ("first" place) and work or school ("second" place). Third places are locations where people easily and routinely connect with one another, have a good time, exchange ideas and build relationships. There have always been "third places" in Des Moines. It's just that no one called them that.

The Butterfly Coffee Shop at 408 Seventh Street created a third place in the 1930s. It also promoted a concept now called "shop local." The Butterfly Café offered "always better food" thanks to the "finest dining products," which the café detailed in its advertisement in the August 20, 1933 issue of the *Des Moines Register*. That "creamy goodness so noticeable in Butterfly malted milks and in the milk served with your meals" was attributed Newens Northland Dairy's perfectly pasteurized milk, which came from the "pick of Polk County herds." Patrons enjoyed that "favorite of ice cream—it's Flynn's, of course, the ice cream that all Des Moines prefers." Guests could also enjoy Schlitz products at the Butterfly Coffee Shop. "It's logical that this famous eating place should serve these famous products supplied by the Des Moines Bottling Company," the café stated.

In the 1930s, the Butterfly Coffee Shop at 408 Seventh Street promised "always better food," thanks to local products like milk from Newens Northland Dairy, produced by the "pick of Polk County herds." *Author's collection.*

Years later, other restaurants in Des Moines would also strive to create a third place by emphasizing their Iowa ties. "Here's Johnny's," which promised "fine food at family prices," offered a gathering place for local women's groups and other patrons after it opened in 1971 at 5501 Douglas Avenue near the Merle Hay Plaza. It was named for Johnny Carson, who was born in Corning, Iowa, and became the king of late-night television, hosting *The Tonight Show* for three decades.

Here's Johnny's was not Carson's idea. It came from Gilbert "Gibby" Swanson Jr., one of the scions of the Swanson food company that introduced TV dinners in the 1950s to the American public. Swanson approached Carson with the idea of an Omaha-based restaurant chain bearing Johnny Carson's name. It would serve typical American food with a Johnny Carson touch, such as the "Carnac Burger," named after one of Carson's signature characters, Carnac the Magnificent, an all-seeing seer in a feathered turban.

Carson lent his name to the project but little else. He was neither the owner of the business nor a stakeholder. He was board chairman, a job that was "mostly for publicity purposes," according to the *Omaha World-Herald.* There was initially much excitement about the opening of the chain, but the restaurants, including the one in Des Moines, were short-lived. By the end of the 1970s, the company was bankrupt.

Other restaurants that opened in Des Moines around this time fared much better, including Beggar's Banquet. This was a deli ahead of its time. It became a Des Moines institution for thirty-five years, first in the Drake neighborhood and then downtown at 1301 Locust Street. The deli offered inspired sandwiches for vegetarians and meat eaters alike in a laidback atmosphere, but Beggar's Banquet closed for good in 2007.

Hungry yet? Let's delve into the fun world of diners, drive-ins, cafés and buffets to rediscover more "third places" that brought Des Moines together.

LONNIE'S, MILLIE'S, CARHOPS AND PORK TENDERLOINS

As the top producing pork state in America, Iowa has long boasted restaurants where guests can savor all things swine. Of all the pork entrées that Iowans crave, however, the tenderloin is king—specifically the breaded pork tenderloin sandwich. It consists of a trimmed and pounded-tender slice of pork loin that's battered, fried and sandwiched in a bun. This is no ordinary sandwich. These are slabs of juicy pork the size of hubcaps placed inside a standard bun, creating a contrast that would be downright ridiculous if it weren't so darn delicious.

In Des Moines, one of the most popular places for tenderloins was Millie's Drive-In. "Oh lord, the many, many times my high school friends and I ate at Millie's after our shifts at the River Hills Theater," wrote Rich Selzer on the "Lost Des Moines" Facebook page.

It was the kind of place you could afford, even as a high school or college student on a limited budget. And, oh that taste! Just ask Lisa (Lamberto) Albright, a Des Moines native who now lives in Lytton, Iowa, and spends her winters in Arizona. "Millie's was always one of my favorites for yummy pork tenderloin sandwiches," said the 1973 Dowling High School graduate. "I remember being in the hospital for several days with hepatitis, and the first thing I wanted my Mom to get me was a pork tenderloin from Millie's! Now I'm craving a pork tenderloin. We don't see those in Arizona."

Millie's (located on Second Avenue just north of downtown) wasn't the first drive-in to serve pork tenderloins in Des Moines, nor was it the first drive-in. Before Millie's, there was Lonnie's Drive-In, which was located at 1175 Second Avenue by the early 1950s. Lonnie's signage outside the

Lonnie's Drive-In included carhops and promoted "The Biggest Tenderloins in Town" for thirty-five cents each in the early 1950s. The restaurant later became Millie's Drive-In. *Author's collection.*

restaurant promoted "The Biggest Tenderloins in Town" for thirty-five cents each.

In the July 13, 1953 edition of the *Des Moines Tribune,* Lonnie's ran an ad seeking carhops, as did two other restaurants: the Les Phillips Drive-In at Sixty-Third and Grand and Coxey's Drive-In at 6001 Fleur Drive. (The ads stated, "Must be over 21, good salary.")

Around this time, Millie and Elwin Husted purchased Lonnie's Drive-In from Lonnie Conner. Back then, it was strictly carhop service at Millie's. You ate in the car, whether you ordered a tenderloin sandwich or a rib dinner.

The Husteds owned Millie's Drive-In until 1973, when they sold it to new owners. After Millie Husted died of cancer at age seventy-four in 1986 (just two years before her former restaurant burned down in 1988), the *Des Moines Register* described her as "the car hop's best friend." Employees remembered Millie's caring spirit and concern for them as individuals—even after they'd gotten into a mustard fight. "Millie walked in one Sunday, and we had mustard all over our face and hair," recalled Ruby Liggett, a former carhop who was quoted in the July 22, 1986 *Des Moines Register* article. "She fired all of us, which lasted about half an hour, I think. She called us back into her office and told us how mustard cost money, and then she laughed about it. That's the kind of person she was."

KING'S FOOD HOST AND THOSE FAMOUS FRENCHIES

If you liked Des Moines's drive-ins, there's a good chance you enjoyed King's Food Host too. This beloved eatery served its famous Frenchies (crunchy, deep-fried cheese sandwiches, sometimes spelled "Frenchees"), which you could order with your meal via the telephones located at each table.

After you checked out the menu, complete with pictures of the food available, you could pick up the phone and order. A short time later, a smiling server would arrive at your table with your food, including Cheese Frenchies and Tuna Frenchies, which could be yours for forty cents and fifty cents each, respectively, back in the day. "I spent a lot of time as a teenager hanging out at King's Food Host eating the Cheese Frenchies," Albright said. "It was so cool to have phones in each booth where you ordered your food."

Anyone who's spent any amount of time at the Iowa State Fair can tell you that nearly anything deep-fried just tastes better. This was true for the Frenchie, according to the clientele at King's Food Host. This was also the place where you could order hamburgers, onion rings, chocolate malts and more, whether you were hanging out with friends after a football game, going on a date or enjoying a quick meal with your family.

After all, King's Food Host was founded as a drive-in restaurant in Lincoln, Nebraska, in 1955 to provide tasty food at a reasonable price. As the chain expanded across Iowa and beyond, it catered to families and starving students in the 1960s into the early 1970s. By 1967, Des Moines had multiple King's Food Host locations, including 1245 Harding Road, 3025

King's Food Host served its famous Frenchies (crunchy, deep-fried cheese sandwiches), which you could order via the telephones located at each table in the restaurant. *Author's collection.*

Douglas Avenue, 2700 Grand Avenue, 1234 Euclid Avenue and 313 Eighth Street, according to advertisements that appeared in local newspapers.

Teens, college kids and families weren't the only ones patronizing King's Food Host. Local business leader John Ruan was often spotted eating breakfast there. "This was a hot spot in Des Moines for 'power breakfasts,'" noted Jim Duncan, a longtime Des Moines food writer.

While the iconic signage topped with a big crown signaled King's Food Host locations across Des Moines and beyond, the restaurant chain's days were numbered. By 1974, the company had filed for Chapter 11 bankruptcy protection. The company hoped to reorganize, but it was never able to return to profitability. King's Food Host restaurants slowly faded from existence.

Cheese Frenchie

6 slices American cheese (American cheese is a must)
mayonnaise
6 slices white bread
1 egg
½ cup milk
¾ cup flour
1 teaspoon salt
crushed corn flakes
oil for deep frying

Make three sandwiches, using 2 slices of American cheese per sandwich. Spread mayonnaise on bread slices. Cut sandwiches on the diagonal into triangles. Combine egg, milk, flour and salt. Dip the triangle sandwiches into egg mixture; coat with corn flake crumbs. Fry in oil at 375 degrees until golden.

BISHOP'S CAFETERIA OFFERED SATISFYING ARRAY OF OPTIONS

If Cheese Frenchies weren't your style, you could always find something more suited to your tastes at Bishop's Cafeteria. This beloved midwestern chain once boasted various cafeterias in Des Moines, including the downtown location at 711 Locust Street, one at Merle Hay Plaza and one on Fleur Drive (and later at Southridge Mall).

Other Bishop's Cafeterias were located around Iowa in Cedar Rapids, Sioux City, Davenport and Waterloo. Benjamin Franklin Bishop started the cafeteria chain in 1920 in Waterloo, according to the blog *My Omaha Obsession*. A post titled "For the Love of Bishop's Buffet: Why, Oh Why, Did They Close?" noted that the Iowa-based buffet chain grew to thirty-five midwestern locations known as the Bishop Buffet and Cafeteria System.

Joy Neal Kidney's mother, Doris Wilson, worked at Bishop's in downtown Des Moines in 1937. The 1936 Dexter High School graduate had a busy schedule, earning money at Bishop's, taking classes and playing basketball for the American Institute of Business (AIB) in Des Moines.

"She eventually dropped out of college because she couldn't afford room rent, but she also realized that the gals who became secretaries had to buy their own clothes," said Kidney, who lives in West Des Moines. "The waitresses at Bishop's were furnished uniforms and two meals a day, so Mom returned to work there during the war years. In early 1943, her brother Dale Wilson stopped by during his last furlough home. The other waitresses were really taken with a man in uniform. When Mom left to go to the train depot with Dale and their parents, they saw members of the Women's Army Auxiliary Corps salute Dale in downtown Des Moines."

Anyone who ever set foot in a Bishop's restaurant knew what an enticing experience it was. The food looked marvelous, from the fried chicken to the mashed potatoes to the chocolate ambrosia pie topped with chocolate curls. With all those choices, it was easy to have eyes bigger than your stomach. "If you lived in one of Iowa's smaller cities or towns and traveled to Des Moines, Bishop's Cafeteria was always a must," said John Busbee, a southeast Iowa native and current host of KFMG Radio's weekly *Culture Buzz* in Des Moines.

As you passed through the cafeteria line with your tray, attendants wearing matching uniforms were ready to help. Kids looked forward to receiving a balloon from the employee at the cash register. "I remember eating there during the 1950s, when they gave each child a balloon with cardboard 'feet' holding it up," Kidney said. "My sister, Gloria, always got the chocolate pie with the curl on top."

Cafeteria-style dining defined Bishop's Cafeteria, which appealed to people of all ages. People still remember the fried chicken, mashed potatoes and chocolate ambrosia pie topped with chocolate curls. *Author's collection.*

The dining room offered a comfortable, inviting place (complete with a fireplace) to savor a meal with family and friends. No detail was overlooked, including clean ashtrays on every table to accommodate cigarette smokers.

Bishop's boomed at a time when cafeteria-style dining thrived in America in the post–World War II era. These restaurants offered affordable meals, appealed to a family clientele and were viewed as a place to eat after church on Sunday or a destination for out-of-town guests.

"I was fortunate enough to attend the All-State Chorus, back when it was held at the KRNT Theater in Des Moines," said Pegg (Willis) Havens of Storm Lake, who graduated from Lake City High School in 1970. "Our high school music teacher, Audrey Williams, made that experience unforgettable. We lunched at Bishop's Buffet downtown and had a special dinner at Noah's Ark restaurant. I felt so grown up being in the big city."

Even Duncan Hines approved of Bishop's. Long before his name was associated with cake mixes, Hines became one of America's leading food writers of the late 1930s into the early 1950s. His claim to fame was his hugely successful *Adventures in Good Eating* guide, where he annually updated the names and locations of restaurants from coast to coast that earned his rigorous seal of approval.

Bishop's Cafeteria, whose advertisements proclaimed "good, refreshing, healthful food," noted that its restaurants were "recommended by Duncan Hines." Bill Bryson cited Duncan Hines and Bishop's in his lively memoir *The Life and Times of the Thunderbolt Kid*, which describes his youth in Des Moines in the 1950s. "Bishop's was the finest restaurant that ever existed. Everything about it was divine—the food, the understated décor, the motherly waitresses in their gray uniforms who carried your tray to a table for you and gladly fetched you a new fork if you didn't like the look of the one provided."

The friendly service left a lasting impression on people. "We have a handicapped son, and the Bishop's employees would carry his tray and make him feel like a normal person," said Dolores Horton on the "You Know You're a Southsider If You Remember…" Facebook group.

Each table at Bishop's had a little light on it that customers could switch on if they needed service, Bryson recalled, "so you never had to crane around and flag down a passing waitress. You just switched on your private beacon, and after a moment a waitress would come along to see what she could help you with. Isn't that a wonderful idea?"

Bishop's also had a "large and highly regarded" assortment of penny candies by the cash register, Bryson recalled. "You could also get a comparatively delicious licorice treat known, with exquisite sensitivity, as nigger babies—though no one actually used that term anymore, except my grandmother."

The discount chain Kmart bought the Bishop's chain in 1983 before selling it in 1988. The new owners slowly began shuttering the various Bishop's locations in the 1990s and 2000s. While Bishop's restaurants are now just a memory, many Iowans feel lucky to have enjoyed this culinary experience with family and friends throughout the years and can still taste Bishop's famous Chocolate Ambrosia Pie.

Bishop's Chocolate Ambrosia Pie

1 (3-ounce) package instant French vanilla pudding mix
1 (3-ounce) package instant chocolate fudge pudding mix
2 cups milk
2 cups vanilla ice cream
9-inch graham cracker crust
1 (8-ounce) carton frozen non-dairy whipped topping, thawed
chocolate curls shaved from a 2-pound milk chocolate bar, for garnish

With an electric mixer, combine pudding mixes and milk. Add ice cream; beat until just thickened. Pour mixture into graham cracker crust. Top with whipped topping. With a potato peeler, shave part of the chocolate bar onto top of pie. Chill pie before serving.

KNOX CAFÉ NEVER LACKED FOR BUSINESS

Homestyle comfort food also reigned at the Knox Café, a mainstay on the east side of Des Moines for decades. Called "the best little restaurant in Des Moines," the Knox Café opened in 1936. Located on East Euclid Avenue, the Knox Café was operated by Charlie Knox and was open twenty-four hours a day, six days a week. It was situated at the junction of four highways (known back in the day by the numbers 6, 64, 65 and 69).

The Knox Café was a mainstay in east Des Moines for decades. It was open twenty-four hours a day and was said to have the best hot beef sandwiches in Des Moines. *Author's collection.*

Advertisements promised diners that they could "come as you are" to enjoy "Iowa's finest, moderately priced, quick service restaurant," along with ample parking and air conditioning.

The Knox Café was said to have the best hot beef sandwiches in Des Moines. Guests also loved the steak and eggs, ham steaks with cherry sauce, turkey, hamburgers, fried fish, grilled cheese sandwiches, chili, butterscotch malts and other diner food, as well as favorite desserts like cherry cream pie and Mrs. Knox's famous cheesecake.

"I remember it as a café to go to after football games at East High School," recalled Joyce Fenton Lewis on the "Lost Des Moines" Facebook page. "I was always aware that we [my family] couldn't eat out often, but when we did—two or three times a year after church—we went to Knox Café, because it was affordable for a family of six."

Patrons who stopped by in the morning could count on a hearty breakfast. "Morning," however, didn't mean 7:00 a.m. for band members playing gigs in the area into the wee hours of the morning. Morning usually meant 2:00 a.m. for these musicians, as well as energetic young people who stopped by for a bite to eat after a night at the movies, bar hopping or Friday night stock car races at the Iowa State Fairgrounds. "Steak and eggs with tomato juice at 2 a.m.," wrote one former Knox Café guest on the Facebook group page. "Great memories!"

If you wanted a bite to eat at that time of the day, it was either the Knox Café, the Toddle House on Grand Avenue or the Y-Not Grill, which had been located at 1323 Sixth Avenue in Des Moines since the 1940s. (The Y-Not Grill might have offered the most colorful dining experience. "That wasn't always the best part of town," noted Jim Duncan, who remembered street walkers hanging out at the Y-Not Grill.)

Knox Café waitresses were known for memorizing customers' orders and verbally conveying them to the cook. "The waitresses would go to a microphone near the kitchen and call out their orders," noted Max Smith, who worked at the Knox Café counter and shared some of his memories on the "Lost Des Moines" Facebook page. "When done, the cook would call out that order to be picked up. I have no idea how the waitresses remembered an order that could include as many as eight to 10 people. I do know the ladies who worked at the time I was there were there for many years."

Instead of itemized tickets, the waitresses used pre-printed cards with numbers around the edges. They would punch one number for the dollar amount, another for the cents. If the total bill reached a dollar amount higher than the pre-printed cards could account for, the servers wrote the total on the back of the ticket, Smith added.

Des Moines native Daniel Finney recalled the Knox Café in his column "The Older I Get, the More I See the Des Moines That Was," which appeared in the *Des Moines Register* in 2016. "Each time I approach East 14th Street at East Euclid Avenue, I expect to see the brown sign for Knox Café displaying the current time with the words Air Conditioned in white letters at the bottom," wrote Finney, who used to eat there on Friday nights in the late 1970s with his parents.

He recalled Helen Burley, a Knox Café waitress who reminded him of Flo at Mel's Diner in the classic CBS sitcom *Alice*, which ran from 1976 to 1985. Helen "always promised to get me home in time to watch my 'green man,' as she called the Hulk," wrote Finney, referring to one of his favorite Friday night TV shows, *The Incredible Hulk*. "She said it with a wink. A wink! Nobody winks anymore. It's probably a felony."

Nevertheless, Helen always made good on her promise. The Knox Café was the place where Finney first tasted rainbow sherbet, served in a tin dish that made a *tink* when the spoon hit the side. Sometimes Finney got to take home an extra goodie from the candy counter when his dad bought him a pack of Freshen Up gum with a liquid center filled with cinnamon flavor.

But all that's gone now. The Knox Café was torn down in 1995. Helen Burley died in 2009. "But sometimes, when I squint, it's still there, and I can almost smell the fried chicken with steak fries," Finney said.

TODDLE HOUSE OFFERED TWENTY-FOUR-HOUR SERVICE

While it's common today for some restaurants and convenience stores to stay open twenty-four hours, that wasn't the case sixty years ago. Classic diners like the Knox Café were among the few places where you could grab a bite at any time, day or night. These twenty-four-hour joints were the most prevalent in larger cities and areas where factory workers were on the job around the clock.

Beyond the Knox Café, one of the few twenty-four-hour eateries in Des Moines was the Toddle House at 2120 Grand Avenue. The Toddle House opened on May 25, 1938, as part of a chain of restaurants operated by National Toddle Houses of Memphis, Tennessee. The Des Moines location became the sixty-first unit in the chain, noted the *Des Moines Register* in 1999.

This quaint restaurant, which occupied a cozy, cottage-style building, attracted people from many different walks of life. As retired *Des Moines Register* columnist Walt Shotwell once described it, "The publisher sat next to the paper boy. The coal tycoon's daughter chatted with the grocery boy, while her date from the New England prep school burned." It was a place where rich and poor were on neutral territory.

The café, which was known for prompt service and sparkling clean surroundings, became the place to be after a ritzy gathering at the Wakonda Club or a local high school dance. About a dozen stools lined the counter, and the crowd at times was three deep as people enjoyed hamburgers on toasted buns, waffles and chocolate pie.

The Toddle House became a favorite of Bill Bryson when he was growing up in Des Moines in the 1950s. After dining "quietly and contentedly" at Bishop's Cafeteria on a Friday evening with his mother, the pair would stroll over to one of the three "great and ancient" downtown movie palaces—the Paramount, the Des Moines or the RKO-Orpheum. After taking in a flick like *The Blob* or *Invasion of the Body Snatchers*, Bryson and his mother would stop by for pie at the Toddle House, "a tiny, steamy diner of dancing grease fires, ill-tempered staff and cozy perfection on Grand Avenue," Bryson wrote.

The Toddle House was little more than a brick hut consisting of a single counter with a few twirly stools, Bryson added, but "never has a confined area produced more divine foods or offered a more delicious warmth on a cold night." Bryson was convinced that he grew up with the smoothest, most mouth-pleasing banana cream pie at the Toddle House. "The pies—flaky of crust, creamy of filling, and always generously cut—were heaven on a plate."

It wasn't poor-quality food, Des Moines's expanding suburbs or the growing number of fast-food restaurants that triggered the Toddle House's demise. Rather, it was the ordinances passed by the City of Des Moines in the 1960s that prohibited parking on Grand Avenue, noted the *Des Moines Register*. Sadly, there was no place for parking on the fifty-square-foot lot. The only place to park was on the street. Fewer patrons went to the café as a result, forcing the restaurant to close in 1970.

STELLA'S BLUE SKY DINER DUMPED MILKSHAKES ON DINERS' HEADS

Some of Des Moines's most beloved diners were a throwback to an earlier era. Stella's Blue Sky Diner was a Des Moines original when it opened in the skywalk level of Capital Square downtown in 1988. The 1950s-style diner featured lots of chrome, Elvis music, Green River soda fountain drinks, Velveeta burgers and malted milkshakes.

It became an instant tourist attraction that hosted everyone from presidential candidates to high school basketball teams from across Iowa who were in town for the state tournaments. Patrons stood in line for up to half an hour just to get a seat during the lunch hour, reported the *Des Moines Register*.

Many people bought malted milkshakes just to see their waitress climb onto a chair or the back of their booth and pour the concoction into a glass balanced on top of the customer's head. (In some cases, the shake was poured directly into the person's mouth.) Even more amazing, few seem to recall the stunt going awry.

President Bill Clinton stopped by the downtown Stella's location in April 1995 to eat with Vice President Al Gore, U.S. Department of Agriculture secretary Dan Glickman and Leon Panetta, who was Clinton's chief of staff. "He came, he talked, he ate 'neutron fries,'" stated the April 30, 1995 edition of the *Des Moines Register*, which noted that Clinton was in central Iowa in the wake of the bombing of the Alfred P. Murrah Federal Building in Oklahoma City to speak at the National Rural Conference in Ames. "Clinton remembered Stella's milkshakes and ambiance from an earlier visit—though he can't have a shake because of an allergy," noted the newspaper. "But he was able to help finish the fries drenched in a spicy cheese sauce."

Stella's opened a second location at 3281 100th Street in Urbandale in 1995. Both restaurants closed abruptly in 2002, according to a 2008 *Des Moines Business Record* article. Stella's in Urbandale relaunched in 2003. "The

Stella's Blue Sky Diner opened in the skywalk level of Capital Square downtown in 1988, followed by a second location in Urbandale. Waitresses poured milkshakes into glasses balanced on their customers' heads or right into the person's mouth. *Courtesy of Jonathan Postal.*

thing about owning your own restaurant business is that you're married to it; you have got to be there," owner Kerri Foster told the *Business Record*. "You have to coddle it and help it along, and teach it to walk. You have to love it. If you don't, then you'll never survive."

Unfortunately, Stella's took another nosedive and closed the doors in November 2007. While owners hoped the third time would be the charm in 2008, Stella's in Urbandale eventually closed forever. People who wanted to own a piece of nostalgia, à la Stella's, could browse a Seeburg 222 jukebox, two 1950s Philco televisions, vintage chairs, tables, signs and other memorabilia sold during a two-day tag sale in August 2011.

PORKY'S DINER HOSTED BIKE NIGHTS, CLASSIC CAR CRUISE-INS

Nostalgia for the 1950s also drove Porky's Diner, another Des Moines original that fans called "indescribably cool," thanks to bike nights every Thursday and classic car cruise-ins on Wednesday and Saturday nights. "It was all about classic American muscle cars, and everyone had their spot," recalled Darren Brown, who runs Nostalgic Enterprises, a classic car shop in Valley Junction in West Des Moines. "Corvettes were parked along the south, while Mustangs were in another area."

All the action was outside on those warm summer nights, Brown added. The Porky's crew would grill burgers, bratwurst and hot dogs outdoors and serve the food on the patio area, along with fries, soda pop and beer. "In the summertime, Porky's was the place to be," he noted.

This place really did get its start in the 1950s as a drive-in, although Porky's Diner was a more modern creation that started in the 1980s and came into its own in the 1990s. While the original location was at 4444 Douglas Avenue (at the intersection of Beaver Avenue), Porky's Diner had expanded to three locations by the year 2000, including 3301 East Euclid Avenue and 1480 Eighty-Sixth Street in Clive. The Douglas Avenue location proved to have the most staying power of the three, thanks to its popular bike nights, classic car nights and unforgettable food, including breaded pork tenderloins.

Porky's Diner attracted a diverse crowd. "Every now and then, a Des Moines–area motorcycle gang can be seen roaring through town on their Harley-Davidson motorcycles—a blur of denim, black leather and tattoos," noted the article "Coppers on Choppers," which ran in the July 21, 2000

From the 1980s into the 2000s, people flocked to Porky's Diner on Douglas Avenue for its 1950s drive-in flair, complete with bike nights and classic car cruise-ins during the warmer months. *Courtesy of Darren Brown.*

edition of the *Des Moines Register*. "Other motorists may take them for outlaws. If only the people of Des Moines knew the gang's 'secret'—its 25 members are a mixture of police officers, firefighters and sheriff's deputies."

The "Wild Pigs" got together every month, with several meeting every Thursday night, at Porky's Diner on Douglas Avenue to discuss motorcycles, upcoming rides and more, the article added.

The end of an era came in 2009, however, when Porky's Diner on Douglas Avenue was razed to make way for a Hy-Vee grocery store that would never be built.

POPPY'S PLACE SERVED UP FOOD, FUN AT ADVENTURELAND

One big piece of Des Moines–area nostalgia that continues to reinvent itself is Adventureland, the amusement park that first opened in Altoona, just east of Des Moines, in 1974. While the park still offers a variety of food options, none is quite like Poppy's Place. Ads from the 1970s called Poppy's Place "the most unusual gastronomical experience of a lifetime."

A 1970s postcard from Adventureland in Altoona called Poppy's Place "a gathering place for young and old where you may enjoy superb cuisine and your favorite beverage in an atmosphere of Iowa antiques." *Author's collection.*

The décor at Poppy's Place was unlike any other restaurant in the Des Moines area at the time, thanks to its eclectic mix of antiques, stained glass and barn siding with knotholes. (Remember, this occurred years before this became a popular trend at chain casual dining restaurants in the 1990s and 2000s.)

In the 1970s, Poppy's Place served cocktails on quilted calico placemats that matched the restaurant's calico cloth napkins. Poppy's featured drinks like the Main Street Special, an iced gin concoction, and a rum-based mix called the Adventureland Express. Both were priced at $2.50 each (that's about $13 in today's dollars), and you got to keep the glass.

The menu at Poppy's Place was varied enough to fit any palate or pocketbook. If you wanted to eat lighter or save some money, you could get a hardboiled egg for $0.25 or a Monte Cristo sandwich served with "Poppy's Taters" (large slices of deep-fried potatoes) for $2.50. If you wanted to go all out, you could try a New York strip steak for $8.75. (That steak dinner is roughly $47 in today's money.)

Other options at Poppy's Place, which was open on Adventureland's Main Street daily from 10:00 a.m. to 11:00 p.m., included smoked pork chops with sauerkraut, filet of red snapper with a Creole sauce and Lobster "Brewer's

Style" for $6.95, which featured generous chunks of lobster fried in a special beer batter served with butter and cardinale sauce (a creamy, buttery affair that can be accented with herbs and garlic).

For more basic tastes, Poppy's Place also served peanut butter and jelly sandwiches and ten-cent coffee. "Just being there is half the fun; eating there is the other half," noted Dennis Allen, who wrote about his experiences in the "What's Cooking?" section of the *Des Moines Sunday Register* for the September 29, 1974 edition. "It makes you comfortable, whether you are entertaining heavy business cronies, dear friends (and there is a difference), or your children."

While the Poppy's Place of the 1970s is just a memory now, the fun continues at Adventureland, which is still going strong. The amusement park was welcoming more than 600,000 visitors annually by the time it celebrated its fortieth anniversary in 2014.

CHAPTER 8

Eat, Drink and Be Merry

From Ronald Reagan to Ruthie

Y ou can't tell the story of lost Des Moines restaurants without revisiting some of the bygone bars that were once part of the city's dining and drinking scene. Some of these places became famous thanks to Ronald Reagan.

Ronald ("Dutch") Reagan lived in Des Moines for a few years in the 1930s before he became a movie star, governor of California starting in 1967 and president of the United States in the 1980s. When his career as a sports announcer brought him to WHO Radio in Des Moines in the 1930s, he was known to patronize long-forgotten restaurants and watering holes like Cy's Moonlight Inn, a speakeasy at Seventy-Third and University.

It was all a big adventure for a midwestern kid like Reagan, who was just trying to get ahead in life during the Great Depression.

Born in Tampico, Illinois, in 1911, Reagan grew up in the small town of Dixon, about one hundred miles west of Chicago. After graduating from Eureka College in Illinois, Reagan landed an announcing job at radio station WOC in Davenport, Iowa, where he did play-by-play broadcasts of Iowa Hawkeye football games for five dollars per game. WOC later sent him to Des Moines to cover the annual Drake Relays. By 1933, Reagan had become chief sports announcer for WOC's sister station, WHO in Des Moines.

During his WHO career, Reagan "announced" Chicago Cubs baseball games in the Des Moines studio by reading barebones results from a Western Union ticker, noted the Des Moines Public Library. He was so skillful that some listeners believed that he actually was at the game.

Long before he was president of the United States, Ronald Reagan was a sports broadcaster at WHO Radio in Des Moines. He and his friends patronized Cy's Moonlight Inn in Windsor Heights. *Courtesy of WHO Radio.*

During his time in Des Moines from 1933 to mid-1937, Reagan lived in a house that had been converted to apartments near the current site of Hy-Vee Hall downtown, noted the Des Moines Public Library. When he wasn't working at the radio station, Reagan hit the town. "He liked to whoop it up," recalled Jack Shelley, a former newscaster and journalism professor at Iowa State University who was quoted in "Dutch Reagan's Des Moines' Days: A Colorful Interlude" in the June 6, 1980 edition of the *Des Moines Tribune*.

If you mentioned Reagan's name to anyone in town who knew him back then, the name "Moonlight Inn" would come up. The Moonlight Inn was a tavern run by the late Cy Griffiths at the southwest corner of Seventy-Third Street and University Avenue. The Moonlight Inn's attraction was a Prohibition marvel known as "spiked beer," near-beer generously laced with straight alcohol.

"It sounds pretty horrible now, but it seemed pretty good at the time, with a kind of smoky taste that was downright addictive," noted the *Des*

Moines Tribune article. "Besides, that's all there was, and the fact that it was illegal added to its charm." "Near beer" was a fermented malt beverage. It was a pale approximation of real beer, but it enabled some breweries like Anheuser-Busch and Miller to weather the difficult years when beer was banned in America.

Back in those Prohibition days in Des Moines, you'd get a carload of your friends, drive out to the Moonlight Inn, buy your spiked beer for twenty-five cents a bottle and drink it in the car or simply stand around. The Moonlight Inn was eventually expanded to include booths and a dance floor. "A generation of parents who thought they were sending kids to Drake University actually were putting them through the Moonlight," noted the *Des Moines Tribune*.

Although Reagan was not yet a movie star, he was a local celebrity by virtue of being on the radio. "Next to spiked beer, Reagan was the Moonlight's top attraction," the *Tribune* article added.

There were rumors that Reagan closed his late-evening broadcasts with a code. "If he said one thing, it meant he would be at the Moonlight Inn in Windsor Heights shortly," the *Des Moines Tribune* article explained. "If he said something else, it was a message to his friends that he wouldn't be there at all." True or not, friends say it would have been like ol' Dutch to do something like that.

The Moonlight Inn wasn't Reagan's only haunt. The swanky Club Belvedere was a close second. Located at 615 High Street in Des Moines, the nightclub had been the former Grant Club near St. Ambrose Cathedral. (By the early 1900s, the Grant Club was the largest men's club in Iowa, as well as the best known and most politically influential. The club's origins were Republican, and the club was named after President Ulysses S. Grant, according to Drake University.)

"In Reagan's heyday, Club Belvedere was strictly class. It even had a chorus line. Illegal booze, of course. And—wow!—a casino," noted the *Tribune*.

Darrell Kiddie, a nephew of Al Kiddie, one of the club operators, recalled that Reagan showed up at Club Belvedere almost weekly—with many different girls. One of the girls Reagan took to the Moonlight Inn and Club Belvedere was Jeanne Tesdell, a Drake graduate he met in early 1936. "We just went for the floor shows [at Club Belvedere]," said Tesdell, who remembered Reagan as a "terrific extrovert." "He didn't drink much, and I never saw him gamble."

Reagan arrived in style after he bought a new, metallic brown Nash convertible for $600 in 1936. "He looked very nice in it—and he knew it," Tesdell told the *Tribune*.

Those who were friends of Reagan back then were adamant about two things: Reagan was careful about who he dated, and he drank so moderately that he was often called on to drive others home. He effectively served as a designated driver long before anyone had heard of the term, noted Lou Cannon, author of the book *Governor Reagan: His Rise to Power.*

Reagan also focused on staying in excellent physical shape. A former lifeguard, he swam regularly in the summer at the Camp Dodge pool north of Des Moines and is said to have rescued one or two swimmers there. While in Iowa, he joined the U.S. Cavalry Reserves at Fort Des Moines on the city's south side in 1937. It was a decision Reagan called "one of the smartest things I ever did," according to Cannon. In one month, he was promoted from private to second lieutenant, noted the American Legion. Reagan would later say that it was in Des Moines that he discovered a lifelong love for horses and riding.

Another Reagan trait that emerged clearly in Des Moines was the fact that he cared about people. He had little time for bureaucracy, recalled Myrtle Williams, a friend from his Des Moines days. She told the story of an impoverished mother who came to WHO Radio's studios seeking food and clothing for her children during those desperate Depression years. She was told to try the local Community Chest (now the United Way) office. She said she already had but was turned away. The discouraged woman turned and left the WHO office. When Reagan heard her story, he got into his car, found her and took her shopping. "Many people thought Dutch had no deep feelings about these things, but he did," Williams told the *Tribune* years later.

Big changes would soon transform Reagan's life. In 1937, Reagan traveled to Los Angeles with the Chicago Cubs in connection with his radio job while the team was there for spring training. He jokingly mentioned to Joy Hodges, a Des Moines native who was working in the movie business in California, that he would like to get into the business too. Hodges arranged a screen test with the Warner Bros. movie studio. By the time Reagan, twenty-six, returned to Des Moines by train, a six-month, $200-a-week contract with Warner Bros. was waiting in his mailbox.

In the next three decades, Reagan appeared in more than fifty movies and got involved in politics, growing more conservative in his political views. He officially became a Republican by the early 1960s and was elected governor of California for two terms in the late 1960s and early 1970s.

Reagan never forgot Des Moines. Friends sent him the old Moonlight Inn sign when the joint was torn down in the 1970s. Reagan displayed the vintage sign in the recreation room of his home in California for years.

Left: The Moonlight Inn wasn't Reagan's only haunt during his years in Des Moines from 1933 to 1937. He also frequented Club Belvedere, a swanky night club at 615 High Street. *Courtesy of WHO Radio.*

Below: President Ronald Reagan's famous words—"Mr. Gorbachev, tear down this wall!"—are preserved on the large stone marker at the corner of Fourth Street and Court Avenue, just blocks from where Reagan lived in the 1930s. *Author's collection.*

When Reagan ran for president, the July 31, 1980 edition of the *Daily Chronicle* in Dekalb, Illinois, ran the story "Reagan in His Iowa Days." It mentioned how "friends of the Republican presidential candidate can still visualize themselves lounging in the west side tavern with the wavy-haired sportscaster having a Prohibition-era 'near beer.'"

After Reagan became the fortieth president of the United States in 1981, he played a pivotal role in helping end the Cold War. In June 1987, he gave one of the most celebrated speeches of his presidency. Standing before the Brandenburg Gate and the Berlin Wall, Reagan challenged Soviet leader Mikhail Gorbachev to create a new era of freedom in Europe. Reagan's famous words, "Mr. Gorbachev, tear down this wall!," are preserved forever on a large bronze and stone marker that was installed at the corner of Fourth Street and Court Avenue in downtown Des Moines in 1999, just blocks from where Reagan lived and worked during those long-ago days of the 1930s.

THE ONE AND ONLY RUTHIE: A DES MOINES LEGEND

Reagan wasn't the only celebrity to emerge from Des Moines during that era. By the 1950s, a Des Moines bar owner named Ruthie (Fontanini) Bisignano had become a national sensation for her unusual barkeeping skills. Ruthie could balance a beer glass on each of her 48DD breasts, fill the glasses and deliver them to wide-eyed customers without spilling a drop. Pictures of her performing that feat appeared in newspapers and magazines all over the world, including the *Stars and Stripes* military newspaper.

In the Facebook group "You Know You're a Southsider If You Remember…," Lyle Spilman noted that when he went to boot camp in San Diego, California, the cab driver asked him where he was from. "When I said Des Moines, the cabbie asked, 'Do you know Ruthie?'"

Ruthie gave a whole new meaning to the term "beer bust" back in the days when beer was the only alcoholic beverage that taverns in Iowa could sell legally. It was Ruthie who charged nearly three times as much for a bottle of beer as other taverns—and customers couldn't get enough. And it was Ruthie for whom a pair of mountains in Korea were named "the Ruthies," thanks to Korean War soldiers.

Necessity—and an offhand remark—inspired Ruthie's unique beer-serving style. It started when Ruthie was running a tavern at 1311 Locust Street. The place was really packed one night. A man sitting at the bar saw

Des Moines bar owner Ruthie Bisignano became a national sensation in the 1950s. She could balance a beer glass on each of her 48DD breasts, fill the glasses and deliver them to customers without spilling a drop. *Courtesy of Chuck's Restaurant.*

how busy Ruthie was and told her she needed another pair of hands. A woman who was with him just laughed. "She doesn't need another pair of hands," she quipped. "She's got a pair of something else that will do the job just as well."

Ruthie agreed. "She propped a couple of glasses up there, and I filled the glasses with beer," Ruthie recalled. "And you know what? I never spilled a drop." Ruthie denied that she ever had wax, paraffin or any other substance injected into her breasts to strengthen their carrying capacity. "'Everything was just me,'" she told former *Des Moines Register* reporter George Mills.

Lest you assume that Ruthie was all boobs and no brains, think again. Connie Wimer, owner and chairman of Business Publications in Des Moines, remembered Ruthie running a tavern on Keosauqua Way. "Ruthie was a really good businesswoman," recalled Wimer, who has lived in Des Moines since 1950 and was inducted into the Iowa Women's Hall of Fame in 2007. "She was in control and took advantage of her assets, even though it was considered racy at the time."

Ruthie Stood Out in a Crowd

Ruthie in her prime was quite a gal. "I've been married 16 times, but only to nine different men," Ruthie told the *Des Moines Tribune* in 1976, adding that one former husband was a member of the Mafia. "You see, honey, I married some of them twice—and one of them three times."

One of Ruthie's marriages ended after just sixteen hours when Ruthie woke up to find her new husband going through her purse looking for her safe deposit key, Mills noted in his book *Looking in Windows: Surprising Stories of Old Des Moines*. Ruthie clarified things (in her own way) when she spoke to the *Tribune*. Ruthie said that Frank Bisignano was the only man she ever married in church, "so he's the only one who really counts."

Frank Bisignano was just a "little-bitty man—five feet tall and that's with his shoes on," Ruthie added. "But he's smart and he's a hard worker and I love him. Frankie wants me for me. All the others were just interested in how much money was in the cash register."

By the late 1950s, Ruthie had largely dropped out of sight after operating taverns at a number of locations around Des Moines. Since then, rumors had circulated that she was shot to death by a former lover, killed in a car accident or living with a rich husband in some far-away city.

All this prompted the *Des Moines Tribune* in 1976 to answer the question, "What is Ruthie doing these days?" Turns out she was living a quiet, happy life on Des Moines's south side at 315 Dunham Avenue with her husband, Frank, who worked as a clerk for an electrical supply company. Ruthie, in her fifties at the time, was no longer working, "except to take care of Frankie," she told the newspaper.

"But Ruthie still stands out in a crowd," the article noted. "And the part that stands out the most is what made her famous as the beer-balancing barmaid of Des Moines during the 1950s."

"I've always been a 48DD, even when I was thin," said Ruthie, who said she could understand how some of the wild rumors about her life got started. She did have several brushes with death. She had been married to some wealthy men. But there was one rumor Ruthie wanted to squelch immediately. "I had a hysterectomy, honey, not a mastectomy," she told the *Des Moines Tribune*. "And if you don't believe me, you can ask my gynecologist."

Hollywood Took Note of Ruthie

Ruthie shared memories associated with her noteworthy career, the *Tribune* noted, citing the following highlights.

She attended five high schools in Des Moines, including East, St. Joseph Academy (an all-girls' high school that merged with Dowling High School in 1971), Roosevelt, West and North, "but the diploma, when I finally got it, wasn't signed," Ruthie said.

She got a job in Chicago as an exotic dancer. She was married several times and operated bars in Chicago and Omaha before opening taverns in Des Moines. She operated taverns at 1330 Keosauqua Way, 723 University Avenue, 1311 Locust Street, 1457 Keo, 311 Second Avenue and at Sixth and University Avenues.

In the 1950s, before liquor by the drink was legal in Iowa, many Iowa taverns bootlegged whiskey, Ruthie recalled. She never sold anything but beer, however. "I didn't have to sell hard liquor," she told newspaper reporters. "I was getting 50 cents a bottle for beer when other tavern owners were getting only 17 cents a bottle."

The fifty-cent beer idea has been attributed to Cecil B. DeMille, the noted Hollywood film director who stopped at Ruthie's tavern twice. At his suggestion, she raised the price beer from the going rate of seventeen cents a bottle to fifty. "He told me people come in to see me, not for the beer, and I should charge a higher amount," Ruthie said. When she took his advice, business didn't fall off at all, Mills said.

Ruthie said that DeMille told her if she were ever in Hollywood, she should stop in for a screen test. "But he didn't offer to pay for my trip out there," she noted. "And I knew I could make $250 a night [roughly $2,500 in today's dollars] in Des Moines for sure, so why should I throw that away on a maybe thing?"

Ruthie loved working Monday nights through Thursday nights, because that's when traveling salesmen poured into Des Moines, along with their cash. Ruthie could be tough, though, Mills noted. "If someone came to watch and didn't buy any beer, she'd say, 'Put something on the bar besides your elbows.'"

Beyond the beer she sold, Ruthie earned additional cash by selling photos of herself for one dollar, plus another dollar for her autograph and yet another dollar if she added a sassy comment. It wasn't unusual for her to sell a dozen or more pictures a night, she told the *Des Moines Tribune* in 1976.

The January 1954 issue of *Vue* magazine featured a four-page layout of Ruthie, including one photograph with the caption "the Dear of Beer." "They paid me $600 a page for that," Ruthie told the *Des Moines Tribune*. (If Ruthie had that number correct, that's nearly $23,000 in today's dollars.)

Ruthie's photos appeared in a variety of magazines and newspapers across the nation. While her image may have pleased many readers, vocal opponents didn't mince words in their letters to the editor. "We were incredibly dismayed by your publication of that disgusting barmaid picture (showing Ruthie Fontanini of Des Moines balancing beer glasses on her bosom)," wrote Raymond C. Stenger, whose letter appeared in the June 11, 1953 edition of the *New York Daily News*. "For such a family newspaper to print such a shocking exhibition is, to say the least, in extremely bad taste."

Another reader listed only as "a mother from Queens" stated, "Is she out of her mind to do a stunt like that? She reminds me of a cow."

Morals Charges Landed Ruthie in Court

As famous as she'd become for her unique barkeeping skills, Ruthie's run-ins with the law launched her from celebrity to international antihero. At the height of her fame, police in Des Moines raided Ruthie's Lounge at 1311 Locust Street in May 1953. What caused all the trouble? "It was an act so disturbing that two vice officers and a police captain, Louis Volz, made a special trip to see it—as indeed did most of the men in Des Moines at one time or another, or so it would appear," wrote Des Moines native Bill Bryson in his memoir *The Life and Times of the Thunderbolt Kid*.

Des Moines police brought charges of obscenity and indecency against Ruthie, even though she was always fully clothed when she performed her beer balancing act. Municipal Judge Harry Grund dismissed the charges. When measured by the standards of the tavern, where everyone was at least twenty-one, he said her act wasn't indecent and "no worse than the performances seen on television."

Ruthie continued running her taverns and later said one of her biggest thrills was having her picture taken with President Dwight Eisenhower at the Iowa State Fair in the 1950s. The whereabouts of that photo are unknown, Mills reported.

Ruthie would also claim that she and a husband were granted brief audiences with Pope Pius XII and Pope John XXIII while traveling in Rome. She told Pope John XXIII that what she tried to do with her life was make

While she retired years ago, Ruthie regained the spotlight again when the *Des Moines Tribune* ran the front-page story "Ruthie Recounts Her Big Moments" in 1976. *Courtesy of Exile Brewing Company.*

people happy. She said the pope replied, "That is good." She didn't explain what she did back in Des Moines to make people happy, other than to say she was in entertainment.

Ruthie's Legacy Lives On

So how does the legacy of a 1950s woman like Ruthie (who passed away in 1993) fit into a world transformed by the 1960s sexual revolution, the 1970s equal rights movement and the twenty-first-century's Me Too movement against sexual harassment?

To answer that, let's look at the Des Moines restaurant and microbrewery that has kept Ruthie's story alive: Exile Brewing Company. R.J. Tursi opened Exile Brewing in August 2012 on the west end of Walnut Street in a renovated 1930s-vintage warehouse once owned by the Fitch Soap Company. When Tursi began crafting his beers, he knew that the one with mass appeal needed to be called "Ruthie." "The beer is not light bodied; it's got body and character and flavor to it, like Ruthie," he said.

Exile describes "Ruthie" as the world's best-balanced beer, brewed with Munich and Pilsner malt and complemented with German Perle hops. "A tribute to a real Des Moines original and the finest woman to ever serve beer in our capital city!"

Mandy Naglich, a writer for Vice.com, first encountered "Ruthie" when she was on assignment in Iowa. "At almost every bar in Des Moines, there is a very distinct tap handle," she wrote. "It's the marker of one of the most popular locally brewed craft beers in the state, and it depicts a brunette woman balancing two pint glasses on…her breasts. When I saw this little sculpture, I immediately snapped a picture, ready to fire off a disappointed tweet about how people just can't keep boobs out of beer. But, upon commenting on the tap handle to my bartender, she replied, 'You know, she was a real woman, and she owned her own bar right here in Des Moines all the way back in the 50s.'"

Naglich reconsidered her view of Ruthie after learning she was much more than just another pin-up girl. In the 2019 online article "How a Busty, Beer-Balancing Bar Owner Became a Feminist Icon in 1950s Iowa," Naglich described Ruthie as a "consummate businesswoman," noting Ruthie was one of the few women—if not the only woman—who owned and operated a bar in Des Moines in the early 1950s.

Naglich explained how Tursi brought Ruthie's story back into the local spotlight nearly fifty years after Ruthie's Lounge shut its doors. She added that Tursi's popular beer, "Ruthie," sells more than seven thousand barrels each year in Iowa, making it the best-selling Iowa-made beer in the state.

While "Ruthie" was part of Exile's beer lineup from the beginning, the label didn't always have such an empowering look. "[Ruthie] started with more of a pin-up look, but that never felt right, especially as the brand began to grow," Tursi told Vice.com. That's when illustrator Ramona Muse Lambert gave the brew a new look. As Lambert dug through pictures of Ruthie and newspaper clippings that nostalgic customers shared with Exile Brewing, she found an image with smiling women in the background as Ruthie performed her signature move. "It seemed like they were rooting

When Ruthie performed her signature move in the 1950s, some people found it offensive, but many (including women) appeared to be rooting for her. Years later, Ruthie would be called a feminist icon. *Author's collection.*

for her, like they were her friends," said Lambert, who noted that this was a much different vibe than men leering at her.

Ruthie's new design showed her looking at the bottles of beer she was pouring and concentrating on her balance, instead of flirtatiously gazing at onlookers like the first version of the label. Her previous crop top and skimpy shorts were updated to a short-sleeved shirt and belted pants. "This woman was a force, not a helpless creature being watched," Lambert said.

While Exile does get complaints now and then about "Ruthie," the team considers this an opportunity to share the story of the real Ruthie—the epitome of a feminist. "Now, as a beer enthusiast and as a woman in the craft brewing world, that's the feeling I get when I look at a bottle of Ruthie," Naglich wrote. "Believe it or not, it's not about the boobs. I see a powerful woman in her element performing the feat that made her an icon."

CHAPTER 9

Dinner Theaters in Des Moines Mixed Entertainment and Good Eats

Bored? Hungry? There was a time before the internet age when entertainment went beyond sitting at home on the couch, streaming movies online, binge-watching TV shows and eating takeout food. Des Moines served up a unique concept called dinner theater, with entertainment, food and spirits all under one roof—and people loved it.

Des Moines's longest-running dinner theaters included the Ingersoll Dinner Theater and Charlie's Showplace. To some, "dinner theater" conjures up fond recollections of pleasant nights out, a satisfying meal, an entertaining show, drinks and dessert, all for an affordable price. For others, it meant a unique venue to celebrate birthdays and anniversaries. "Dinner theaters were a novel concept in the 1970s," said John Busbee, who hosts the *Culture Buzz* show on 98.9 KFMG Radio in Des Moines every Wednesday.

Before then, few Iowans were familiar with dinner theaters. Iowa at that time offered little in the way of professional theater companies. "I'd never heard of anything like a dinner theater before I went to Charlie's Showplace," said Van Harden, an Adel native who has been a radio broadcaster for nearly fifty years and hosts his own drive-time morning show on WHO Newsradio 1040 in Des Moines.

This new entertainment concept started in August 1953, when six actors from New York bought a run-down tavern in Richmond, Virginia, and turned it into what would become the country's first dinner theater.

In the Midwest, dinner theaters became popular in Kansas City, Omaha (thanks to the Firehouse Dinner Theater in the Old Market district) and the Chanhassen Dinner Theatres southwest of Minneapolis, Minnesota.

Nearly 150 professional dinner theaters were operating around the country by 1976. Let's go back in time to this era, when dinner theaters combined food and fun in Des Moines.

REMEMBERING THE SHORT-LIVED THEATRE FABULOUS

Des Moines's first dinner theater, Theatre Fabulous, opened in early 1973 with the show *Sweet Charity*. The April 13, 1973 issue of the *Des Moines Register* ran the headline "Theatre Fabulous Needs Work." Located in the former Paramount Theater at 509 Grand Avenue, the building had been extensively remodeled to become a dinner theater. "In a world where there is far too much tearing down of old buildings with character to make room for parking lots with none, this is a venture that deserves support," noted writer Nick Baldwin.

Main floor prices, which included both dinner and the show, were $6.00 per single and $11.50 per couple on Monday and Tuesday nights, with prices rising to $9.00 and $17.50, respectively, for Friday and Saturday. Balcony prices (with no dinner) were per $3.00 single and $5.50 per couple on Monday and Tuesday, up to $4.50 and $8.50, respectively, on Friday and Saturday. Perhaps the balcony seats were the best deal of all, however, especially since the dinner theater opened its doors "to a large crowd and considerable confusion," Baldwin wrote.

Because of the way in which the once-sloping main floor was remodeled into tiers to accommodate the dining tables, many audience members could only get glimpses of the stage at best. Baldwin was optimistic that deficiencies like this would be corrected. "Des Moines can use a dinner theater, and it would be nice to see this one make the grade," he wrote, noting that upcoming shows included *The Owl and the Pussycat* and *Guys and Dolls*.

After a few starts and stops and a limited number of shows, Theatre Fabulous closed permanently in 1974.

CHARLIE'S SHOWPLACE OFFERED FINE DINING

Another dinner theater also got its start in Des Moines in 1973, although this one would endure for years. The King Charles Theatre Ltd., better known as "Charlie's Showplace," opened at Fifth Street and University Avenue, just north of what is now MercyOne Des Moines Medical Center, on September 26, 1973, with a performance of the Neil Simon comedy *Barefoot in the Park*.

Tickets to the new dinner theater ranged from $5.95 to $9.95 for the dinner and show. Cocktails and a buffet-style dinner were served from 6:30 to 8:00 p.m., with the show from 8:30 p.m. to 11:30 p.m. Shows were scheduled to run Wednesdays through Saturdays through mid-October 1973.

The creative forces behind Charlie's Showplace included Mariam McKeever and her husband, Larry. The couple had been employed by the Des Moines Community Playhouse in the late 1960s, with Mariam as the children's theater director and Larry as technical director. Both often appeared on the Des Moines Playhouse stage. The couple also began doing

radio and TV commercials and opened Des Moines's first professional recording studio and talent agency, Lariam Associates Inc., at 515 Twenty-Eighth Street in 1968.

While the McKeevers were operating their recording studio, they were asked to produce a play for a new entertainment idea: dinner combined with a show. After three sold-out shows, the McKeevers decided to look into operating a full-time theater of their own. The result was Charlie's Showplace, which was housed in a remodeled Orthodox synagogue built in 1922 at Fifth and University. The unique venue, which included a balcony, could hold approximately 325 people.

Charlie's Showplace was a dinner theater that opened at Fifth Street and University Avenue on September 26, 1973. Audiences received this program for the 1980 comedy *Beginner's Luck*. *Author's collection.*

Mariam served as the producer, director and manager at Charlie's Showplace, which billed itself as an "informal and fun dinner theatre," while Larry was a host, technical director and wine steward. Mariam was a true professional, someone who combined good business sense with a flair for Broadway-style

Charlie's Showplace, which was created by Mariam McKeever (*right*) and her husband, Larry, included a professional acting company and staff that offered five to eight dinner theaters a week for nearly twelve years. *Author's collection.*

entertainment, noted Gary Propstein of Des Moines, who began working at Charlie's Showplace as a teenager in the 1970s.

Charlie's Showplace included a professional acting company and staff who offered five to eight dinner theaters a week for nearly twelve years. "We were making $100 a week, which allowed us to make a living and raise families," recalled Tom Milligan, a Des Moines native who became acquainted with the McKeevers at the Des Moines Community Playhouse. He was also an actor and scene designer at Charlie's Showplace.

The pay and benefits allowed Charlie's Showplace to not only recruit but also retain some of the region's top talent for the dinner theater. "Mariam was a great entrepreneur and really wanted to offer group health insurance," Milligan said. "It wasn't easy to find a company that would provide it, but she worked out a deal with State Farm Insurance by the late 1970s. State Farm had to classify us as 'gypsies,' but we all got health insurance."

When Charlie's Showplace opened, shows had a three-week run. As the dinner theater grew in popularity, shows usually ran for five to six weeks, although blockbuster hits could last even longer. "We were the first theater in Iowa to get the rights to perform *Annie*, which ran eight weeks," Milligan said.

Performances at Charlie's Showplace ranged from classics like *Harvey* to small-cast comedy shows to *Fiddler on the Roof*, which the venue produced three different times. The cast also performed at least one melodrama per year, plus Charlie's offered some children's theater productions from time to time.

In some ways, entertainment at Charlie's Showplace was ahead of the curve. Consider *On Golden Pond*, which was a play before the movie of the same name was released in 1981. "Charlie's featured *On Golden Pond* before it came out in the movie theaters," Propstein said.

Accomplishments like this helped Charlie's Showplace thrive. "Even though we ended up producing 114 shows during the dinner theater's history, it took a long time to build an audience in those early years," Milligan said. "Once people figured out that they'd get dinner and a show here, though, we sold out the house every single night for eight years."

The meals were just as important as the shows. "No matter the quality of the show, the people sit down to eat first," said Milligan, who has been working professionally in theater for nearly fifty years in Iowa. "You had to have a really great meal and a great show."

Charlie's Showplace was known for its high-quality food and for offering one of Des Moines's premier wine lists. Much of the credit goes to Chef Guido Fenu, who added an Italian flair to the foods he prepared. "Chef Guido was a perfectionist, so the food was always a step above a typical buffet," Propstein said.

Fenu was born on the Italian island of Sardegna (Sardinia). He moved to Berlin, Germany, in 1958, where he learned the art of hotel and restaurant hospitality. He worked in Switzerland; London, England; and New York City before moving to Des Moines in 1964. Fenu worked his way to America by serving on cruise lines, Propstein recalled. That's how Fenu met a Des Moines couple who praised Fenu to local restaurateur Johnny Compiano, owner of Johnny and Kay's on Fleur Drive.

Compiano helped recruit Fenu to Des Moines, where this talented chef began a successful catering service that served various clients, including Charlie's Showplace. Since the dinner theater didn't have its own commercial kitchen, Fenu cooked the food off site and brought it to warming ovens at Charlie's Showplace.

Fenu's famous buffets would include roast baron of beef and a second entrée ranging from veal to chicken. Fenu carved the meat himself. "I loved Guido's prime rib," said Propstein, who noted the Des Moines Embassy Club still uses Fenu's prime rib cart, which was imported from Italy.

Charlie's Showplace patrons also loved Guido's mostaccioli salad featuring tubular-shaped pasta and Italian flavors. "Anytime he removed it from the buffet and served something else in its place, people always noticed and asked him to bring back the mostaccioli," Propstein said.

People would always ask Fenu for the recipe, he added. Fenu would tell them to come to ten shows in a row, and then he'd give them the recipe. If a patron met this requirement and reminded Fenu of their deal, the chef still didn't give up all his culinary secrets. "He'd say, 'I never told them I'd give them the whole recipe!'" Propstein said.

By 1982, ticket prices for Charlie's ranged from $13.75 for the buffet and show on Wednesdays, Thursdays, Fridays and Sundays to $15.95 on Saturdays. Discounts were available for children under age twelve and for senior citizens. If seats were available, show-only tickets could be purchased any night for $8.50. Beverages (other than coffee, tea or milk served with the dinner) cost extra.

The buffet was served from 6:30 p.m. to 8:00 p.m. Wednesdays through Saturdays, with the show starting at 8:30 p.m. On Sundays, the buffet ran from 5:00 p.m. to 6:30 p.m., with the show starting at 7:00 p.m. For Wednesday matinees, the doors opened at noon. "The buffet was on the stage, so designing sets meant creating space where you could remove the buffet," Milligan recalled.

As Fenu's career evolved, he opened the upscale Guido's Restaurant in downtown Des Moines at the Savery Hotel. During the last six months Charlie's Showplace was open, Michael LaValle (who later became the general manager and executive chef of the Des Moines Embassy Club) handled the catering for the shows.

From Charlie's Showplace to his own restaurant, Fenu brought a new level of excellence to dining in Des Moines. "Guido was the frontrunner for good food and wine in Iowa and set the standard for all fine dining in the state," noted his obituary after he passed away in Santa Barbara, California, at age seventy-three in 2013.

❖ ❖ ❖

Mostaccioli Salad

While this isn't Chef Guido Fenu's famous mostaccioli salad that he served at Charlie's Showplace in Des Moines, this recipe offers a way to create your own taste of it at home.

3 cups uncooked mostaccioli (or penne pasta, if desired)
1 medium cucumber, thinly sliced
1 small yellow summer squash, quartered and sliced
1 small zucchini, halved and sliced
½ cup diced sweet red pepper
½ cup diced green pepper
½ cup sliced ripe olives
3 to 4 green onions, chopped
cherry tomatoes, cut in half (use as many as you like)

Dressing
⅓ cup sugar
⅓ cup white wine vinegar
⅓ cup canola oil
1 ½ teaspoons prepared mustard
¾ teaspoon dried minced onion
¾ teaspoon garlic powder
½ teaspoon salt
½ teaspoon pepper

Cook pasta according to package directions. Drain and rinse in cold water. Place in a large bowl; add the cucumbers, summer squash, zucchini, peppers, olives, onions and cherry tomatoes. In a small bowl, whisk the dressing ingredients. Pour over pasta mixture; toss to coat. Cover and refrigerate for 8 hours or overnight. Toss again before serving. Serve with a slotted spoon.

Cocktails, Wine and More

Along with the delicious buffet, guests at Charlie's Showplace could enjoy after-dinner drinks from Brandy Alexanders to Grasshoppers (ice cream cocktails), all for $2.50 a glass in the early 1980s.

Specialty drinks were also extremely popular. Each show had its own signature drink. The 1980 show *Beginner's Luck*, for example, featured the specialty drink "The Novice," although the 1980 program didn't detail what ingredients were featured in the cocktail. The crowd-pleasing "I Do" sundae, named after the musical *I Do! I Do!*, included vanilla ice cream with any of the liqueurs served at Charlie's, from amaretto to apricot brandy to peppermint schnapps.

Propstein learned the fine art of bartending after he started working at Charlie's Showplace at age fifteen in February 1974, first as a busboy and then a waiter. As he washed and dried cocktail glasses, he watched the bartenders make various drinks. He learned from masters like Al Downey, a Black gentleman who served as Charlie's longtime bar manager.

Wines sold by the glass in 1980 at Charlie's included Delicato Burgundy, Rose, Chablis, Giacobazzi Lambrusco and more. Looking for something more unique? Charlie's offered a 1962 Château Margaux, Propstein noted. This Bordeaux wine, which captured the hearts and dollars of wine aficionados, could be purchased for $75 a bottle in Charlie's early days, rising to $150 a bottle by the time the theater closed in the early 1980s.

Charlie's Showplace sometimes offered wine insights in its programs. The May 29–June 29, 1980 program for the comedy *Beginning's Luck* included the article "How Do I Know What I'm Getting?" "One of the frequent questions in a new wine drinker's mind is, 'How do I know whether this is good wine or not?' The answer is, you have to depend on your wine host, your palate and the label. The final judge is, of course, you."

The detailed piece offered the following tips:

In the U.S., traditional names for wines (Burgundy, Riesling, rose) are likely to be the least desirable wines. Wines that feature the name of the grape used (Cabernet Sauvignon, Pinot Noir, etc.) are the most closely controlled, and are generally the best quality American wines.

The finest vintners will not compromise their quality. Once you find a label you trust, in the USA you can be fairly sure that all the varieties of wine under that label will have similar quality. Now, that doesn't mean you will like everything under that label. But it assures you of the quality.

Try until you find what you like. Then occasionally experiment some more. That's the way to decide what your palate thinks is quality.

The program also clarified what was acceptable when it came to smoking at Charlie's Showplace. Smoking was allowed during dinner and intermissions because "at those times we are a restaurant," the program stated. Smoking was banned when the play was on. "Then we are a theatre, and no smoking is allowed."

Charlie's Showplace attracted a unique crowd. While high-profile local business and community leaders like Charles Gabus, owner of Charles Gabus Ford in Des Moines, were regulars, this was no exclusive club. "Everyone went to Charlie's for the same reason," Propstein said. "You were all there as equals."

Who Haunted the Dinner Theater?

Because Charlie's Showplace was located in a part of town that some viewed as a bit sketchy in the 1970s and early 1980s, some people were concerned about their safety and worried that thugs might break into their cars during the show. Mariam McKeever hired off-duty police officers to handle parking lot security and give patrons greater peace of mind.

Charlie's Showplace was housed in the former Beth El Jacob Synagogue, which had been built in 1922. The synagogue served the local Jewish community until the late 1950s, when a fire broke out following a Passover service in 1956 and badly damaged the building. The congregation built a new synagogue across town to the west at 954 Cummings Parkway.

After Charlie's Showplace opened for business in the 1970s in the converted synagogue, former staff members, actors and patrons were convinced the building was haunted. They think the spirit seen most often in the former synagogue was a benevolent Jewish rabbi named Rabbi Naftali Hertz Zeichik.

In 1905, this Lithuanian-born Orthodox rabbi and noted Talmudic scholar became the head rabbi of Beth El Jacob Synagogue, which was the only Orthodox synagogue in Iowa at the time. For more than forty years, Zeichik, who was called the "Chief Rabbi of Iowa," performed weddings across the state. Zeichik remained a prominent rabbi in the Midwest until his death at age seventy-nine in early 1947 at Iowa Methodist Hospital in Des Moines following a short illness.

After Charlie's Showplace opened, various people reported ghostly phenomenon that they attribute to Zeichik. "Rabbi was happiest when the place was full," Propstein said. When Propstein was carrying a tray of drinks in the theater one night, it felt like some invisible force was gently grabbing the tray and shaking it. "It wasn't enough to spill the drinks, but it was enough to let you know someone was there," Propstein said. "I'd say, 'That's enough, Rabbi,' and it would stop."

One day, a new customer stopped by the dinner theater's box office, located at the top of a flight of stairs near the entrance, to purchase tickets. When she asked if she could take a look inside the theater to find her table, the staff assured her that would be fine. When she returned a few minutes later, she asked the lady at the box office, "Who was that older gentleman sitting at the table in the balcony?" She said the man had a funny-shaped beard, an unusual hat and a black coat. The box office lady was stunned, since she didn't think anyone was in the theater at that time. She and the customer stepped inside the theater to take another look. No one was there.

Then there was the time when the electricity suddenly shut off for no apparent reason during a performance of *Fiddler on the Roof* at Charlie's Showplace around 1979 or 1980. After an extended time, the power began flowing later on its own. "Iowa Power and Light Company checked into it but had no idea why that happened," Propstein said.

Even a blind dog that lived in the theater seemed to know that odd things happened there. Larry and Mariam McKeever, who owned Charlie's Showplace, lived in a penthouse at the theater. "The McKeevers' dog would suddenly stop sometimes and act like it was sensing something we couldn't see," Propstein said.

Stage curtains would occasionally blow open for no apparent reason at Charlie's Showplace. This was also the kind of place where the creaky, old wooden floors almost made it sound like someone was walking around on the stage from time to time late at night, even if you couldn't see anyone.

While these things might spook the faint of heart (or simply provide fodder for scoffers), other unexplained events at Charlie's Showplace simply defy logic. Ask Milligan, whose scene shop was located in the lower level of the theater. One day when he went to grab his electric drill, the tool was nowhere to be found. "I had been using it not that long before, so at first I assumed someone had borrowed it," Milligan said.

While he asked his colleagues about the missing drill, no one knew anything about it. Then Milligan figured someone had taken it as a prank. Still, there was no sign of the drill as days turned into weeks. Milligan finally gave up hope and purchased another drill.

Then something stopped him in his tracks. "Almost a year to the day after my original drill went missing, I walked into the shop at the theater and saw that original drill just sitting there, unplugged. I was absolutely shocked." He could never find a rational explanation for how the drill had disappeared and magically reappeared nearly a year later.

INGERSOLL DINNER THEATER STARTED IN A BARN

As Charlie's Showplace gained an audience (including, perhaps, a bit of the supernatural), another dinner theater business in Des Moines was beginning to take shape. Little did a group of high school students and their teachers know that a summer project they started in 1976 would grow into one of the most popular dinner theaters in Iowa.

It sprang from an East High School performance of *The Music Man* in the spring 1976, recalled Propstein, a 1976 graduate of East High School in Des Moines. Teacher/director Charles Carnes told his students that he'd dreamed of having a dinner theater someday and asked the students what they thought of that idea. "Oh, that sounds like fun!" came the reply.

The Purple Cow Players began performing in an old barn on Cutty's Campground west of Des Moines near Grimes. Not only did these ambitious students rehearse long hours, but they also waited tables during performances. After the guests had enjoyed their meal, the Purple Cow Players climbed on stage to sing and dance their hearts out. "We did four shows at Cutty's that summer," recalled Propstein, who added that the Purple Cow Players were based at Cutty's for about a year.

Then people started hearing rumors that the former Ingersoll movie theater at 3811 Ingersoll Avenue in Des Moines was going to be turned into a XXX movie theater. That's when the Purple Cow Players moved from Cutty's, set up shop in the old movie theater and created what would become the Ingersoll Dinner Theater. This new location boasted more seating, larger stage space and a little more room to grow. And grow they did!

Carnes became the producer of the Ingersoll Dinner Theater. He also become an authority on the dinner theater business and at one point served as secretary of the National Dinner Theater Association.

The Ingersoll Dinner Theater grew from offering performances on Friday and Saturday evenings in the summer to performing Wednesdays through Sundays all year long, specializing in musicals and comedies. Audiences were delighted with Broadway musicals standards such as *Oklahoma!* and *The Sound of Music*.

The comedies and musicals performed at the Ingersoll Dinner Theater attracted audience members from across Iowa and beyond. The dinner theater's performers doubled as the servers. *Author's collection.*

The shows typically had four-week runs at the Ingersoll Dinner Theater. The music that accompanied the shows typically consisted of musicians playing a couple of keyboards, percussion and maybe a guitar, recalled John Busbee, who was the group sales manager at the Ingersoll Dinner Theater from 1986 to 1989 and also performed in some of the shows.

The Ingersoll Dinner Theater could hold more than two hundred audience members. Doors opened at 5:00 p.m., with dinner at 6:00 p.m. followed by the show at 7:30 p.m. Shows were performed Wednesday through Sunday, with a matinee on Sunday. "Wednesday and Thursday were good for attracting tour bus groups," Busbee said. "People would come from all over Iowa and all over the country."

The theater's goal of providing quality entertainment benefited not only the theater but also the entire Des Moines area, noted an undated Ingersoll Dinner Theater History webpage at netins.net that appears to date from the late 1990s. "Last year, almost 16,500 people attended the Ingersoll Dinner Theater in groups. Almost 60 percent of them came on buses from out of town. Many of those buses left the Ingersoll only to shop at one of Des Moines' spacious malls or to enjoy the atmosphere and history of other area attractions, such as Living History Farms and the Bridges of Madison County."

By 1989, tickets to dinner and a show at the Ingersoll Dinner Theater could be purchased for less than thirty dollars apiece. (That's roughly sixty dollars today.) "The goal was to provide an enjoyable experience but still make it affordable," Busbee said.

The meals were cooked by Carnes's sister, Sandra, in the Ingersoll Dinner Theater's kitchen in the northwest corner of the building. The buffet included carved meats, potatoes, vegetables, dinner rolls and more. Those who remember the fare have described it in intriguing terms, from "truck stop comfort food" to "high-end church-basement food." No matter what, the options were midwestern at their core, and guests loved it.

Guests were invited table by table to come to the buffet line in an orderly fashion. Sometimes the buffet featured foods that fit the theme of the show. When the Ingersoll Dinner Theater presented the musical *1776*, for example, the buffet included Boston-inspired foods, Busbee noted. Unlike Charlie's Showplace, the Ingersoll Dinner Theater's performers doubled as the servers, he added.

Dessert would be served at intermission, and after-dinner drinks were available for purchase. The Ingersoll Dinner Theater had a bartender to mix cocktails for the guests, said Propstein, who worked at the Ingersoll Dinner Theater for several years in the 1980s after Charlie's Showplace closed.

The Ingersoll Dinner Theater used a lot of local talent. The performers received a small stipend for their work. This didn't mean the performers were unskilled. "There's great talent in Des Moines," said Busbee, who has lived in Des Moines since 1979. "Des Moines has a strong history of actors and musicians who've gone on to regional and national acclaim."

In the early 2000s, when the Ingersoll Dinner Theater presented the musical *Grease*, the *Des Moines Register* gave the Ingersoll's performance a better review than the national tour group that had performed the show at the Des Moines Civic Center around the same time, Busbee noted.

The Ingersoll Dinner Theater wasn't just for adults. The Ingersoll Children's Theater Company formed in 1989 to provide children with the fun-filled experience of live theater.

WHY DID DINNER THEATERS DIE?

While Des Moines audiences loved their local dinner theaters, times changed, and so did business at both the Ingersoll Dinner Theater and Charlie's Showplace. Dinner theaters had begun to fall out of vogue by the mid-1980s as new entertainment venues opened in the city. "When Charlie's opened, there weren't a lot of entertainment options in Des Moines at the time," Milligan said. "The KRNT Theater had been torn down, and the Civic Center wasn't open yet."

Limited entertainment opportunities hadn't always defined downtown Des Moines. Des Moines once had a thriving nightlife, especially in the 1930s and 1940s. A new burst of energy came in 1946, when the Cowles Broadcasting Company bought the former Shrine Temple Auditorium at the southeast corner of Tenth Street and Pleasant Street. Built as a Za-Ga-Zig Shrine in 1927, this was the largest theater in the Midwest and one of the largest in the world, with a seating capacity of 4,139, noted the Iowa Rock 'n' Roll Hall of Fame.

By the mid-1960s, the KRNT Theater was hosting huge stars like the Beach Boys and Simon and Garfunkel, both of which played to a full house. Other legends who performed at KRNT Theater included the Doors; Chicago; Strawberry Alarm Clock; Blood, Sweat and Tears; Jerry Lee Lewis, B.B. King and more.

By the early 1970s, however, the Cowles Broadcasting Company had shifted its focus from radio to television and sold the KRNT Theater in 1974, according to George Davidson Jr. on DesMoinesBroadcasting.com. By 1985, the landmark KRNT Theater had been demolished.

A major new entertainment venue had become available in the meantime. The Des Moines Civic Center opened its doors in June 1979. With a seating capacity of 2,744, the venue built a reputation as one of the nation's leading theaters to experience a touring Broadway performance, concert or other special presentation.

As technology advanced, it also unleashed a home entertainment revolution, starting in the late 1970s into the 1980s with an array of channels on cable television and the introduction of the video cassette recorder (VCR). All this allowed people to watch shows from the comfort of their own home. This also took a toll on the dinner theater market.

Many dinner theaters nationwide began closing in the 1980s and 1990s. Des Moines wasn't immune. "By the time we closed on December 31, 1984, there were other entertainment options in Des Moines," noted Milligan, who added that Charlie's ticket prices were thirty-five dollars at the end. (That's about eighty-six dollars today.) "We'd created a place where the food couldn't get any better, and the shows couldn't get any better. Times had changed, and so had people's interests. Maybe it was time to take our last curtain call and go, so that's what we did."

The McKeevers sold Charlie's to the Mercy Hospital Medical Center, which used the building for an education center for a number of years. The building was torn down by the early 2000s.

The Ingersoll Dinner Theater would last an additional twenty years after Charlie's closed, but the final curtain call came in 2004. In early October 2004, Des Moines's local CBS News affiliate, KCCI, reported that the Ingersoll Dinner Theater was closing after twenty-eight years in business. Owner Charles Carnes blamed the closure on financial problems, noted KCCI, which added that the business had been one of the oldest dinner theaters in the country.

Today, only a handful of dinner theaters remain across the country. Yet the thrill of the dinner theater won't soon be forgotten. "I do a lot of

The Ingersoll Dinner Theater was located in a former movie theater for many years. While the final curtain call came in 2004, the building still stands on Ingersoll Avenue. *Author's collection.*

speaking around Iowa, and it's amazing how many people still remember Des Moines's dinner theaters," said Milligan, who works with Humanities Iowa to provide one-man plays showcasing prominent Iowans from years past, including artist Grant Wood and ag editor/politician Henry A. Wallace.

There's just something magical about seeing a production in person, John Busbee added. "I'm a strong believer in the power and appeal of a live performance."

Chapter 10

Downtown Des Moines and the Revitalization of Court Avenue

While downtown Des Moines was one of the coolest places around by the mid-twentieth century, complete with some of the region's most legendary restaurants and bars, the area fell on hard times as Des Moines suburbs continued to grow in the post–World War II era.

By the early 1980s, the city's core had become a business district by day and more like a demilitarized zone by night. Yet the transformation of Court Avenue, which started in the late 1970s and gained momentum in the 1980s, marked a major turning point for the city. As revitalization efforts reenergized the city in the 1990s and 2000s, the evolution of downtown Des Moines was nothing short of spectacular.

"The city that a legion of presidential campaign staffers and journalists are now swarming over is not the one many of them might recognize from cycles past," wrote Colin Woodward in the Politico article "How America's Dullest City Got Cool," published on the eve of the 2016 Iowa caucus. "No longer just a drab dateline from the first battleground state, this metropolis is riding high in the polls."

Woodward noted that Des Moines in recent years had been named the nation's richest (by *U.S. News*) and economically strongest city (Policom), as well as the best city for young professionals (*Forbes*), families (Kiplinger), home renters (*Time*) and businesses and careers (*Forbes*).

Woodward, who was stunned by Des Moines's metamorphosis, didn't mince words describing "old Des Moines." "The capital of Iowa has long had a reputation as one of the least hip, least interesting and least dynamic cities in the Western world, a dull insurance town set amid the unending corn fields of flyover country, a place Minneapolis looks down on and the young and ambitious flee as soon as they graduate."

But unbeknownst to many outside the Midwest, Des Moines had transformed during the past fifteen years into "one of the richest, most vibrant, and, yes, hip cities in the country," Woodward acknowledged. "Its downtown—previously desolate after 5 p.m.—has come alive, with 10,000 new residents and a bevy of nationally recognized restaurants."

DOWNTOWN DES MOINES, FROM CLASSY TO SEEDY

Modern Des Moines reflects the downtown area's ability to come full circle. In the late nineteenth and early twentieth centuries, downtown Des Moines was the hub of commerce and retail activity in the city, anchored by flagship department stores like Younkers.

But the growth of the suburbs and more transportation options by the mid-twentieth century created challenges for Des Moines and other urban centers across the nation. Even before Interstate 235 was built through the Des Moines metro, opening in stages between 1961 and 1968, hardly anyone lived downtown, even though thousands of people worked there.

By the late 1960s, the heart of Des Moines had become little more than an office park for the city's leading industries, including insurance and government. The decline of downtown Des Moines eroded the dining and entertainment scene in the heart of Iowa's capital city. On Friday and Saturday nights, teenagers raced their cars through the empty streets, circling the downtown loop from Grand to Locust Avenue over and over again.

By the 1970s, downtown Des Moines was far from a family-friendly place or a desirable option for meeting friends for drinks or dinner. The Court Avenue area, for example, had become a seedy district distinguished by run-down hotels, flophouses, brothels, XXX movie theaters and other dubious "attractions."

When the August 18, 1974 edition of the *Des Moines Sunday Register* ran a huge advertisement on page 4B for the new Altoona amusement park called Adventureland, another ad placed just to the left of the theme park ad promoted the Theatre Mini-X at 214 Fourth Street. The sketch of a woman tossing back her long, flowing hair as her mouth appeared to utter a seductive moan drew attention to XXX films like *Whatever Happened to Miss*

September and *Marriage and Other 4-Letter Words*, which were showing at the downtown theater.

The story "Dining Out in the Big City," which appeared in the March 2, 1979 edition of the *Des Moines Register*, seemed to acknowledge that much of downtown Des Moines was less than enticing, except, perhaps, to high school sports fans from Iowa's small towns. "Downtown Des Moines takes a lot of flak most of the year. But when the basketball tournaments hit town (girls next week, the boys the week after), the city's central area comes alive with thousands of excited teenagers, proud parents, frantic fans and tense coaches….Many of the teenagers descending on Des Moines come from Iowa's small towns for a rare trip to the big city. And they're looking for places to eat and things to do that can't be found back home in Ackley or Hudson or Glenwood—or wherever you're coming from."

The *Register* visited eight downtown restaurants that could offer something different than people might find in most of Iowa's smaller towns. The article started with Old Market Spaghetti Works on Court Avenue, with its family-friendly, informal feel. "Its 'concept style' décor, sprinkled with hanging stained glass panels, advertising memorabilia and packing-crate dividers, is an ideal spot for basketball fans looking for lots of cheap food at cheap prices in a fun atmosphere."

Noteworthy highlights of the restaurant included a ticket cage reception area, blackboards posting current wines and "even a genuine 1936 firetruck that serves as a salad bar." The menu wasn't complicated, the article continued, featuring spaghetti with one sauce or a combination of any of seven different sauces (including a meat sauce, a white clam concoction and a beer-and-cheese mixture reminiscent of Velveeta and Budweiser).

While Old Market Spaghetti Works wasn't praised for having the most convenient location, it did offer an average price of $3.95 per dish (that's the all-you-can-eat cost). "The restaurant is not close to Vets," the article noted, referring to Veterans Memorial Auditorium where the high school basketball tournaments were played. "But if you plan on trekking down to J.C. Penney's anyway, you'll be right in the neighborhood."

Among the other downtown restaurants on the *Register*'s shortlist were the Midtown Chinese Restaurant (928 Sixth Avenue, where wonton soup was $1.95 for dinner); King Ying Low ("this Chinese restaurant relies on the food, not the décor, for its Chinese flavor," stated the article, with the "usual selection" of Cantonese dinners ranging from about $2.25 to $4.95); the Soup Kitchen at 810 Walnut Street ("If soups, salads or sandwiches featuring cheeses, fruits and vegetables appeal to you, the Soup Kitchen is the place to go.…If any kind of meat is what you're looking for, don't bother, because they don't serve it"); and Pickle Barrel No. 2 (a downtown delicatessen selling kosher, with cheese on rye for $1.35).

"These and other good restaurants are bound to be packed during peak hours, so allow plenty of time to eat and get back to the auditorium [Veterans Memorial Auditorium] in time for tip-off," the article added.

SKYWALKS AND THE MAGIC OF MAID-RITE

By the early 1980s, city leaders were trying to enhance downtown Des Moines by installing an enclosed system of skywalks above the street that allowed people to walk from building to building in climate-controlled, glass corridors. Des Moines took a cue from Minneapolis, which installed the first modern skywalk system in 1962 as a potential solution to help its downtown area recapture some of the retail business it had lost to suburban shopping malls starting in the late 1950s.

In 1981, Des Moines began constructing its multimillion-dollar skywalk system, which opened to the public in 1982. New restaurants began to pop up due to the skywalk system, including Stella's Blue Sky Diner, a 1950s-themed attraction that opened in the 1980s on the skywalk level of the Capital Square building.

The skywalks also connected people to the Kaleidoscope at the Hub, a downtown shopping mall and food court built in 1985. The mall started in the 500 block of Walnut Street and continued to the 600 block of Walnut Street. At its peak, the multistory mall had about thirty retail stores, as well as a third-floor food court accented with neon signs promoting Taste Spuds, Sally's Old Fashioned Hamburgers, Panda Chinese Foods, JJ Jasmine Thai Cuisine and Iowa's legendary Maid-Rite, the king of the loose-meat sandwiches.

The story of the Maid-Rite began in 1926, when Fred Angell, a meat cutter in Muscatine, Iowa, developed a recipe with just the right combination of ground beef (with a specific grind size and meat/fat ratio) and a distinctive seasoning featuring Fred's unique blend of spices. When a deliveryman tasted Fred's new creation, he exclaimed, "This sandwich is made right!"

With that, the Maid-Rite legend was born. "The Maid-Rite recipe has stayed the same from the beginning," said Bradley Burt, president and CEO of the Maid-Rite Corporation based in West Des Moines. "There's no other sandwich like ours."

Call it the king of the loose-meat sandwiches. Maid-Rite is an Iowa classic, and the chain used to have a restaurant in the Kaleidoscope at the Hub mall in downtown Des Moines. *Courtesy of Maid-Rite.*

What started as a small Maid-Rite restaurant in Muscatine grew into one of America's first quick-service, casual dining franchise restaurants. One of the biggest Maid-Rite fans of all would have to be Jim Zabel, the beloved sportscaster whose career spanned nearly seven decades at WHO Radio in Des Moines. Before his passing in 2013, the iconic radio personality and ultimate Iowa ambassador served as the Maid-Rite spokesman. He even made a commercial for Maid-Rite, complete with a riff on his high-energy slogan, "I love 'em, I love 'em, I love 'em!"

"Maid-Rite is truly part of Iowa's culture," Burt said.

COURT AVENUE AND THE KAPLAN HAT COMPANY

While city leaders hoped that amenities like skywalks and downtown malls with food courts would help spur a renaissance of downtown Des Moines, critics charged that these developments only furthered the abandonment of street-level retail.

Before contemporary, cool restaurants and other amenities would grace downtown Des Moines, things as unglamorous as a tax credit, construction equipment and hard hats were required to spark the revolution. Just ask Des Moines developer and restaurateur Bruce Gerleman, who became the first Iowa developer to use new historic tax credit legislation to revitalize old buildings and bring them back to life.

After starting with the Crawford Mansion and other historic buildings on Grand Avenue in Des Moines, Gerleman set his sights in 1983 on the Homestead Building downtown at the corner of Third and Locust Streets.

At the time, the property, which had been built in 1893, was so far from being up to code that the city condemned it. It was a far cry from its glory days as a publishing company where the famed Wallace family of Iowa produced their farm magazines. It later became the Hotel Martin, where popular WHO Radio broadcaster Ronald Reagan stopped by the bar occasionally in the 1930s. By the early 1980s, however, the building had been abandoned, although an empty casket stood in the front window.

Gerleman restored the historic Homestead Building and opened the refurbished property in 1984. That was the first use of tax credits for historic renovations in downtown Des Moines. He opened The Metz, an exclusive, white-tablecloth restaurant known for its French cuisine that would serve the community for twelve years. (In 1998, Gerleman opened his new restaurant, Splash Seafood Bar & Grill, in this location to offer Des Moines a fine dining seafood restaurant.)

In 1983, Gerleman also began buying up Court Avenue properties that had fallen into disrepair. In a year's time, he purchased eleven properties.

Bruce Gerleman used historic tax credits to revitalize the Homestead Building at the corner of Third and Locust Streets. It housed The Metz restaurant before Splash Seafood Bar & Grill opened there in 1998. *Author's collection.*

Many of the buildings he bought were notorious—a biker bar, flophouses, several gay bars, the Blue Nude with its peep shows and a brothel were among them. "I helped the gay bars move to the east side," said Gerleman in a 2017 interview with local food writer Jim Duncan. "They are still there."

The most eccentric building on Court Avenue was the Saddlery Building, which was stacked to the rafters on five floors with 250,000 hats of all kinds. Buying the building from the older Jewish couple who owned the place and had been in the hat business meant buying all those hats too. "I ended up paying nearly $400,000, and two thirds of that was for hats," Gerleman said.

A month-long hat sale turned into a national phenomenon after *The Today Show* ran a segment about it. "Truckers and cowboys were coming in from all over the country," Gerleman said. "I took cash only and sold most hats for $5, $10 and $20. I stuffed the money in hat boxes. In a month, I paid the entire building off with hat sale money."

It was just one more fascinating chapter in the history of this distinctive property. The Saddlery Building at 307 Court Avenue had been built in 1881 by Mr. J. Rubelman of Muscatine, Iowa, who decided that Des Moines, with its two rivers and thirteen railways, would be advantageous to his thriving saddlery company. He was right and ran a successful saddle, harness and leather works there for almost twenty years.

Since then, the building had also been home to a shoemaker, a rubber company, a stove manufacturer, a glove company, the Krispy Kone Company and the Kaplan Hat Company, which Russian immigrant Elisha Kaplan established after he moved to Des Moines in 1898.

The Kaplan Hat Company was thriving by the 1920s. A news brief in the January 1, 1928, edition of the *Des Moines Register* noted, "The Kaplan Hat Company reports better business in 1927 than in 1926 and 1925, with prospects for a healthy increase in 1928. The concern is making felt hats, a new product, and plans to employ 16 more people, now having 20 on the payroll."

The company became a wholesaler of hats and caps of all sizes and styles. The hats provided the perfect theme for the Kaplan Hat Company restaurant, which Gerleman opened in the mid-1980s. When the November 8, 1986 issue of the *Des Moines Register* ran the story "His Hat Company Is Now a Restaurant: Filled to Brim with Memories," staff writer Gene Raffensperger detailed what it was like for former Kaplan Hat Company manager Harry Gold to eat at the new restaurant housed in his former workplace. "'My office was right here,' Gold said, pointing just inside the restaurant doorway and pointing to an area that now serves as the bar." "Today, the place designs and sells such things as Maui melt sautéed vegetables and chicken marsala," added the article. "It is art deco, upscale and definitely draws a yuppie crowd at midday."

The article noted that Mr. Gold ordered a Reuben sandwich, a salad with French dressing, coffee and pineapple sherbet the day he took at first look at the new restaurant. "Has the building changed? Of course. Kaplan Hat Company—the hat company—had five floors. The restaurant occupies what amounts to two and a half floors. There is dining in what was the basement; the bar is on the main floor and the there is more dining in what amounts to a deck halfway between the main floor and old second floor."

There were also hats and pictures of hats that weren't around when hats were the business of the Kaplan Hat Company, the article added. "For one thing, said Gold, the firm did not deal in women's hats. 'Right here where we're sitting, there would have been boxes of hats stacked on top of tables,' said Gold. 'The ceilings in this place were 15 feet high. The boxes would have been almost to the ceiling.'"

By 1989, the *Des Moines Register* noted that "the frenchee, a classic grease-feast, gets a snazzy treatment as an appetizer at Kaplan Hat Company, but the star of the menu is pork scallopini." The news brief in the October 26, 1989 issue added that entrees ranged from $3.95 to $14.95 at the restaurant, which was open from 11:00 a.m. to 3:30 p.m. and from 5:00 p.m. to 1:00 a.m. Monday through Saturday, as well as from 10:00 a.m. to midnight on Sundays. Major credit cards were accepted, and highchairs were available. There was no nonsmoking section, and the restaurant wasn't accessible to the handicapped.

Honey-Mustard Pork Scallopini

Pork scallopini can be made in a variety of ways, from an entrée with a creamy lemon sauce to mushroom and marsala sauce. This version, which honors the spirit of the Kaplan Hat Company, offers a tasty way to get a delicious meal on the table fast.

4 boneless butterflied pork chops (4 ounces each)
2 tablespoons honey
2 tablespoons spicy brown mustard

⅓ cup crushed Ritz crackers (about 8 crackers)
⅓ cup dry bread crumbs
1 tablespoon canola oil
1 tablespoon butter

Flatten pork to ⅛-inch thickness. In a small bowl, combine honey and mustard; brush over both sides of pork. In a shallow bowl, combine cracker and bread crumbs; add pork and turn to coat. In a large skillet, cook pork over medium heat in oil and butter for 2–3 minutes on each side or until crisp and juices run clear.

DOWNTOWN AND COURT AVENUE, PAST AND PRESENT

From the 1980s to the early 1990s, Court Avenue saw a number a new restaurants and bars open, including Jukebox Saturday Night, which Gerleman opened in 1985 at 212 Third Street. It was a showstopper, with gold records on the sidewalk and a portion of a 1957 Chevy car protruding from the wall.

Other hot spots downtown included Gringo's and Julio's. Located at 308 Court Avenue, Julio's offered Mexican-inspired food, live music and more. People still recall Julio's delicious chili, jalapeño poppers, chicken nachos, queso burgers, taco salads, enchiladas, one-dollar margaritas, Long Island iced tea and Sunday night jazz performances.

The downtown area even became home to the Des Moines Grand Prix. For one weekend every year from 1989 to 1994, racecars could be seen zipping through city streets in an attempt to win the top prize. Drivers drove a total of sixty-six laps (118.8 miles) around the 1.8-mile course, with an average speed of 61 miles per hour, according to the blog TopTenDesMoines.com. The late local business titan John Ruan sponsored and helped create the event, which was broadcast on ESPN. The race course snaked through downtown and crossed the Des Moines River on the Grand Avenue and Locust Street Bridges. Spectators lined the skywalks to watch cars pass below, noted the *Des Moines Register*.

Left: The revitalization of historic Court Avenue included Julio's at 308 Court Avenue. Julio's offered Mexican-inspired food, including jalapeño poppers, chicken nachos and margaritas, along with Sunday night jazz performances. *Author's collection.*

Below: Revitalization efforts that started in the 1980s have transformed downtown Des Moines into a vibrant urban center. Court Avenue, an entertainment district, has included a variety of restaurants, including Spaghetti Works (shown here in 2019). *Author's collection.*

The downtown district suffered tremendously, however, during the massive Flood of 1993, which devastated Des Moines that summer. More than 19 feet of water inundated the Kaplan Hat Company building, for example. The trouble began July 8, when eight to ten inches of rain fell in the upper Raccoon River watershed. On July 9, the levee was closed, noted the Des Moines Water Works. At 1:00 a.m. on July 11, water started pouring over the levee. The Raccoon River crested at the historic level of 26.75 feet, which was 1.75 feet higher than the levee.

At 3:02 a.m. on July 11, 1993, the Des Moines Water Works shut down operations after the water treatment plant and general office were inundated with floodwater. The National Guard air-lifted equipment in and out of the water treatment plant. Seven days later, the Des Moines Water Works began pumping potable water from the Fleur Drive plant. Customers could use the water for sanitary purposes on day twelve, and the water was safe to drink on day nineteen.

Downtown Des Moines was forever changed by the Flood of 1993. The 1993 Des Moines Grand Prix was canceled. While the race was held again in 1994, it wasn't able to make up for the financial loss from the previous year, leading to the permanent end of this unique event. The Flood of 1993 also put the Kaplan Hat Company restaurant out of business. The ground level of the building was left vacant until 1996, when Court Avenue Restaurant & Brewing Company started to move in its brewing equipment.

While many restaurants didn't survive the devastating Flood of 1993, others would open up in the area in later years. Today, the Court Avenue district and downtown Des Moines remain a vital, dynamic part of the city.

Chapter 11

Savor a Taste of the Iowa Caucus

You can't talk about Des Moines's restaurant history without noting how food and politics go together in Iowa, especially in Iowa's capital city. Des Moines becomes ground zero for the national and international media every four years in February, when the Iowa caucus takes place.

Much has been written about "why Iowa" when it comes to the caucus. Oxford-educated politician Richard Acton put it this way: "My theory is that America is like an airplane with its wingtips in New York and Los Angeles. Those extremes plunge and soar, but the body in the middle stays relatively stable, and Iowa is in the middle of the middle."

The Iowa caucus offers unparalleled access to the nation's leaders and presidential candidates. Since the early 1970s, Iowa voters have had an exceptional role to play in determining who will become America's next president. "The Iowa caucuses have created a vibrant political atmosphere unlike any other in the world," noted Rachel Paine Caufield, author of the 2016 book *The Iowa Caucus*.

While Iowa doesn't pick the president, the Iowa caucus narrows the field of candidates who are just at the start of a long journey. When the media descends on Iowa every four years to cover the caucus, restaurants across Des Moines and Iowa make the news just slightly less often than the presidential candidates. It's enjoyable for the restaurateurs as well. "The whole world comes to Des Moines for the Iowa caucus," said Chef George Formaro of Des Moines.

Formaro was an eighteen-year-old employee working at the City Grill in Des Moines when he saw Connie Chung, the well-known reporter who became the first woman to co-anchor *CBS Evening News*. She was in town to cover the Iowa caucus. "I was star-struck," he said. "It was one of the most exciting parts of my early cooking career."

Sometimes the local chefs themselves become the focus of attention. It wasn't uncommon for Formaro and his team to see presidential candidates in the dining room after the restaurateurs opened Centro in downtown Des Moines in 2002. "More amazing, though, is the time when Peter Jennings was in town to cover the Iowa caucus," said Formaro, referring to the former anchor of *ABC World News Tonight*. "He stopped by to eat at Centro and wanted to introduce himself to me."

It's not uncommon for local chefs and caterers to build long-term relationships with media outlets that cover the Iowa caucus every four years. Lisa LaValle, a chef and owner of Trellis, a restaurant at the Des Moines Botanical Center, has catered for CBS News for more than sixteen years. "The Iowa Caucus is a positive impact, and the media are generally good to work with," she said.

They tend to request casual food they can eat on the go, but they prefer an Iowa twist, such as a sandwich with Iowa-raised bacon or a salad with sweet corn. "Iowa food reflects the pride and care we take with our meals," said LaValle, who catered a New Year's Eve party a number of years ago for Bill and Hillary Clinton at Capital Square in downtown Des Moines.

WHAT EXACTLY *IS* A CAUCUS…AND WHY IS IOWA FIRST?

So, maybe you're still wondering, "What exactly is the Iowa caucus?" A caucus is a meeting of supporters or members of a specific political party or movement. While Iowa has long had a caucus, it wasn't until 1972 that this system gained national prominence.

The tumultuous 1968 Democratic Convention in Chicago exposed deep divisions within the party. Fred Harris, then chairman of the Democratic National Committee, appointed a committee to address these problems. That commission recommended policy changes to make the party's nomination procedures more transparent and inclusive.

Among the recommendations was a rule that delegates to the national party convention would be chosen in a way that allowed open participation at the local level. Meanwhile, the Iowa Democratic Party had already crafted a system of local caucuses. The four-step system allowed all party voters to participate in small-scale local meetings (precinct caucuses) and elect delegates to county conventions. At the county convention, party voters would elect delegates for a convention representing all counties in a Congressional district. At the district convention, party voters would elect delegates to a statewide convention, at which delegates to the national convention would be selected. "And so it was that in 1972… Iowa had the first contest to select party nominees for the presidency," Paine Caufield wrote.

The Iowa caucus didn't generate much interest outside of the state, however, until a little-known southern governor, Jimmy Carter, came along. Carter had neither the money nor the name recognition to launch a viable national presidential campaign in 1976. He opted to focus on Iowa, hoping to outperform the other candidates and draw national media attention. Carter campaigned heavily in the state, using one-on-one meetings so voters could get to know him. His investment paid off, propelling him to the White House.

Right from those early years, food and politics were intertwined in Iowa, especially in Des Moines. "When Jimmy Carter took his Cinderella campaign for president to Iowa in 1975, he opened his office at Babe

Since the early 1970s, Iowa voters have had an exceptional role to play in determining America's next president. During the Iowa caucus, political candidates, international media professionals and others dine in restaurants in Des Moines and beyond. *Author's collection.*

Bisignano's Italian restaurant [in downtown Des Moines]," noted the article "Iowa Restauranteur Rides Caucus Crest," which appeared in the October 25, 1987 issue of the *Orlando Sentinel* newspaper.

"They needed a place to take mail and didn't have the money for a real office," recalled Bisignano, who was seventy-four years old at the time of the interview. "His [Babe's] generosity was a smart move," wrote reporter Craig Crawford.

Carter's unexpected Iowa victory made Bisignano as famous among Washington insiders as any restaurateur in the nation's capital, the article noted. "The former New York boxer relishes talking politics with the consultants, reporters and presidential candidates who camp out in his downtown restaurant during years divisible by four," reported the *Orlando Sentinel*. "As the Iowa Caucus gained influence, so did Bisignano."

In 1984, Bisignano had to juggle service for two presidential candidates at once. "Aides for [Walter] Mondale and [Gary] Hart called to say they were coming over, so I staggered them about 30 minutes apart," Bisignano told the *Orlando Sentinel*.

A TASTE OF THAILAND: SERVING THE "PUBLICS"

Just as reporters covering the Iowa caucus couldn't resist interviewing a colorful restaurateur like Bisignano, they also loved stopping by the Taste of Thailand in downtown Des Moines during the 1980s to get the answers to all the big questions. Have you ever seen a bird fly backward? Are you able to touch your toes? Whom will you vote for? All this and more defined A Taste of Thailand, which conducted polls on all sorts of topics with people who were hungry for discussion and Thai food.

Thai natives Prasong "Pak" Nurack and his wife, Benchung "Beni" Laungaram, opened their popular restaurant in December 1983 in an abandoned auto repair shop, repainted bright yellow. "So the publics will know we are here," Pak said.

It may have been the only restaurant in the world with a homemade voting booth. The quixotic T.O.T. Polls (Taste of Thailand) and the delicious Thai food practically made A Taste of Thailand a mandatory stop for presidential candidates and reporters.

Years before Pak opened Des Moines's original Thai restaurant, and decades before Pak would become a Thai national senator, he ran a diner

Iowa—Community Style

In January 1992, Prasong "Pak" Nurack, in the cook's apron, and Friends of A Taste of Thailand celebrated the successful campaign to save the restaurant from the urban renewal wrecking ball. Photo by Bob Mandel

A Taste of Thailand: Serving the "Publics"

is a randomness to nature and to the farmer's life. Corn and soybean harvests were poor in 1993, bountiful in 1994, and weak last year. Spring rains made plantings late — or canceled them. Perhaps as many as 200,000 acres weren't planted. Then it became deadly hot in August, mischievously cold in September. Corn harvests were about half of 1994's levels.

♦ ♦ ♦

And so that is it. Iowa is about the land and nature and people and taking pride in what we do with our lives. But it is also about gorging yourself on blueberry strudel in Pella, on three kinds of sausages in Amana, and the very best fried pork-tenderloin sandwich in the world. It is about remarkable steak houses, each with no windows: Jesse's Embers in Des Moines, Lark Supper Club in Tiffin, and Rube's in

Reporters covering the Iowa caucus in the 1980s and early 1990s loved stopping by A Taste of Thailand in downtown Des Moines, where owner Prasong "Pak" Nurack (shown here in the cook's apron) ran informal polls covering politics and more. *Author's collection.*

on Court Avenue called Little Joe's. Thai cuisine was a new thing in Des Moines when Pak and his wife introduced their native food on weekends at Little Joe's.

In the late 1970s, most Iowans knew little about southeast Asian cuisines, noted Jim Duncan, a food writer from Des Moines. Iowa governor Robert D. Ray drew Iowans' attention to this part of the world when he courageously welcomed hundreds of Tai Dam refugees to Iowa in the 1970s as they fled their home country at the end of the Vietnam War.

Pak also opened up a whole new world for Iowans through his cuisine. He was a big personality who could easily talk people into trying something new and different, first at Little Joe's and later at his family's restaurant in the 200 block of East Walnut in Des Moines.

Pak began capturing media attention in the mid-1980s for his distinctive food and his restaurant's political flair. "Candidates, news organizations and special-interest groups have spent thousands of dollars on polls trying to determine which men Iowa caucus-goers will anoint as front-runners for the 1988 presidential nominations," noted the *Chicago Tribune* in the November 24, 1987 article "Forget Costly Polls: Eat Thai to Find Out Who's Winning Iowa." "They could have saved a lot of money and gotten a good meal in

179

the process by checking out the results posted on a wall of the one and only Thai restaurant in the capital of cornfed beef."

The article noted that Pak, forty-five, was a lawyer who held a master's degree in political science. His bright-yellow restaurant, located in the shadow of the gold-domed state capitol, was frequented by politicos, activists and others lured by the food and informal polls.

Diners at A Taste of Thailand received a ballot with the menu and could vote at their table or in a makeshift voting booth. Ballots were then placed in a box next to one poster showing the most recent results and another that said, "Road to the" and then featured a picture of the White House.

Pak insisted that there was no ballot stuffing. "I tell them to look at the ballot box where it says 'honesty' on it," he told the *Chicago Tribune*. "And I tell them: Please, just one vote." He also supplies real voter registration cards.

With his low-tech sampling process, Pak could be surprising accurate with polling results. "About a week before the most recent CBS–*New York Times* poll and three weeks before the most recent Des Moines Register Iowa Poll, the unscientific sample of diners at the Taste of Thailand restaurant had determined that Sen. Paul Simon (a Democrat from Illinois) and Sen. Bob Dole (a Republican from Kansas) were the choice of the moment in their respective parties," the *Chicago Tribune* noted in 1987. Dole would win the 1988 Iowa caucus on the Republican side, while Simon would finish a fairly close second that year to Representative Richard Gephardt, a Democrat from Missouri.

Three candidates came to call on Pak personally in 1987, including Senator Simon, Senator Joseph Biden (a Democrat from Delaware) and Republican Alexander Haig, the U.S. secretary of state under President Ronald Reagan and the White House chief of staff under Presidents Richard Nixon and Gerald Ford. "But the restaurateur has withheld endorsement, saying he didn't want to influence the poll," the *Chicago Tribune* noted. Pak did say that Haig showed "courage for coming to a restaurant where most of the patrons are liberal and Democrat."

"Nobody Lies"

How did a unique character like Pak come to Des Moines? When he was a lawyer in Thailand, Pak had dreamed of touring America after reading about it in books and seeing it on the news. He moved to Chicago in 1971 to study political science. "I like politics, and you learn that all the players in the world know about politics in the United States," Pak told the *Chicago Tribune*. "I wanted to learn something more."

He worked part time washing dishes at the Rodeway Inn near O'Hare International Airport while he earned his master's degree in political science from Northeastern Illinois University.

While Pak and his wife considered going back to Thailand, they wanted to see what smaller towns were like and headed west from Chicago. "This was the first big town we found," he said of Des Moines. "We decided to stay. It's an agricultural town and instead of rice fields, we see cornfields. That's nice."

Pak and his wife became acquainted with many people in Des Moines. "They are interesting people. We talked issues over and we had something in common." It was during the discussions with patrons that Pak decided to conduct an informal poll of public opinion, partly as a marketing device for his restaurant and partly to keep discussions of current issues alive.

Fascinated by American politics, Pak decided to begin a monthly poll in 1986. He started asking serious and not-so-serious questions, ranging from people's feelings about the Farm Crisis to their favorite pet. The move to presidential politics was a natural next step. "People come here to eat, but they talk about politics," Pak said.

Amazingly, the results of A Taste of Thailand's polls have never been far off from more established surveys. A *New York Times/CBS News* survey released on October 31, 1987, for example, showed that Senator Paul Simon had made a dramatic leap and was edging ahead of the Democratic presidential pack in Iowa for the first time, reported the November 27, 1987 issue of the *New York Times*. "The Taste of Thailand poll showed the same thing a week earlier," Maureen Dowd noted in her article "Iowa Restaurant Serves Up Sweet and Sour Poll Results."

"We get pretty good information," the "ebullient" Pak told Dowd. "Nobody lies."

The newspaper explained how A Taste of Thailand, which featured a cosmopolitan beer list of 259 brands from thirty-six countries, catered to presidential candidates, political operatives, city and state officials, journalists and lobbyists for farm groups. "This," Pak said, pulling out a camera to take a few candid shots of a CNN crew having dinner, "is the same camera that took pictures of Joe Biden and Paul Simon eating here."

During A Taste of Thailand's polls, patrons wrote down their political preferences, either in the privacy of the restaurant's curtained polling booth or in the more convivial atmosphere of their tables.

THAI NETWORK
ชายงานไทย

215 E. Walnut Street
Des Moines, Iowa 50309
Phone 515/282-0044

THIS IS TO CERTIFY THAT

DOUGLAS K. COOPER

HAS COMPLETED ALL REQUIREMENTS AND SURVIVED
THAI'S HOT & SPICY FOOD

For location and recomendation of THAI business
anywhere in U.S. call 1-800-USA-THAI
(over)

While A Taste of Thailand was known for its polls, it was also famous for its hot, spicy food. The restaurant issued cards like this so diners could prove that they could take the heat. *Author's collection.*

While A Taste of Thailand's political polls drew the *New York Times'* interest, Dowd couldn't resist sharing results from the restaurant's general-interest polls. People were interested in talking about reincarnation (37 percent of those polled at A Taste of Thailand believed in it); television shows and talk show hosts (67 percent said they preferred *M*A*S*H* to Johnny Carson); touching your toes (76 percent replied they could do it and 24 percent, presumably out-of-shape respondents, called it a silly question) and where disgraced televangelists Jim and Tammy Bakker will end up (the majority felt that Switzerland, rather than heaven or hell, was their destination).

No matter your opinion on politics or other pressing issues of the day, everyone agreed on two things: A Taste of Thailand's food was great, and it could be *hot.* "Taste of Thailand was the place to be," recalled John Busbee, who hosts the *Culture Buzz* show on 98.9 KFMG Radio in Des Moines every Wednesday from 11:00 a.m. to 1:00 p.m.

While Busbee preferred to stick to chicken and vegetable dishes, adventurous eaters could find plenty of excitement. On the statistically coldest day each year in Des Moines (which usually occurred in February), the restaurant sponsored International Hot and Spicy Food Day. Pak and his team offered a buffet with all the hot food you could eat, along with all the cold beer you could drink. You even had to sign a waiver stating that you knew what you were getting into if you chose to try to the buffet, as if names of foods like "Suicidal Beef" and "Angry Shrimp" weren't a big enough clue. "I enjoy spicy food, but that was way too much," Chef Formaro said.

While Pak eventually moved away from Des Moines, opened another restaurant in Iowa City and later returned to Asia to pursue his political career in Thailand's senate, A Taste of Thailand made a lasting impression on many Iowans.

Oh, that spicy food, recalled Coleen (Hildreth) Myers, who grew up in Lake City, Iowa, and now lives in Ankeny. In the late 1980s, Myers's friend from India married a man from Thailand. Myers became acquainted with the couple at Iowa State University in Ames. She was invited to the couple's wedding at the Episcopalian church in downtown Des Moines, as well as the reception, which included a sit-down dinner at A Taste of Thailand. "It was a very fancy dinner, and I vowed to try everything, but some of it was so hot that one bite was about all I could handle," Myers said. "It was an experience I will never forget."

CHAPTER 12

Changing Times and the Future of Des Moines Dining

I t is one thing to listen to reporters from the coasts describe how Des Moines's dining scene has changed during the years they've covered the Iowa caucus. It's another to hear these changes explained by those who know it best—the people who've lived here for decades, the tastemakers who've broken new ground in the restaurant business and the local chefs who have carried on classic menu options while creating innovative, new dishes.

Some of these changes started taking hold when chain restaurants began to flourish, especially in the suburbs, at a time in the 1970s when the dining experience became about something more than the just the food. The Cork 'N Cleaver, located at 1238 Eighth Street in West Des Moines, got guests talking by presenting its wine list on an empty, oversized champagne bottle.

After reporter Nick Lamberto visited the restaurant in 1973, he wrote "Do-It-Yourself Salads at Cork 'N Cleaver," which ran in the July 29, 1973 edition of the *Des Moines Register*. "A long time ago, a much-traveled newsman told me, 'Never eat in a place where the lights are so dim you can't tell whether you're putting salt or pepper on your food. A lot of places use dim lighting to hide bad food under the guise of atmosphere.'"

Undeterred, Lamberto ordered crab legs for $5.95. The table had no tablecloth and wobbled slightly, he added. The waiters all wore shorts and tennis shoes. The piped-in music was mainly hard rock. "It was hardly conducive to hand holding or intimate conversation," noted Lamberto, who dined there with his wife. He admitted that the food was good, though, including the unique flavor of his wife's twelve-ounce top sirloin, which had been marinated in pineapple juice, soy sauce and burgundy wine. He concluded that the Cork 'N Cleaver "qualifies as a place with dim lights, atmosphere and reasonably good food."

Shopping malls helped usher more chain restaurants into Iowans' culinary consciousness in the 1970s, although not all chains were housed in or near malls. The Rusty Scupper, for example, was located at 2600 Grand Avenue, west of Terrace Hill. For a time, this became one of the hottest destinations in the city among Des Moines's young professionals.

The place conveyed a cool vibe, from the live music to the distinctive tables covered with one-of-a-kind, hand-painted tiles. "It had a huge, sophisticated bar that really conveyed a sense of style," recalled Lisa LaValle, the owner and chef at Trellis, which opened in the Greater Des Moines Botanical Garden in 2013. "It was the place to be seen."

This was also the era when Paul Trostel, who had grown up on a ranch in Colorado, opened Colorado Feed and Grain at 1925 Ingersoll Avenue in 1974. "Colorado Feed and Grain was the local watering hole for the young professionals to go for drinks," noted LaValle, who spent more than twenty years of her career operating a café in the Des Moines Art Center. "It defined itself by the diversity of people who flocked there."

While Colorado Feed and Grain was Trostel's first restaurant in Des Moines, it certainly wouldn't be his last. He successfully owned and operated many more restaurants before opening Trostel's Greenbriar in Johnston, Chips Restaurant in Ankeny and Trostel's Dish in Clive. "When Paul Trostel moved his brand from Ingersoll [Colorado Feed & Grain, Rosie's Cantina] to Johnston in 1987, there wasn't much variety in the local dining scene," noted Jim Duncan, a longtime Des Moines food writer. "In fact, Trostel introduced the appetizer menu at Colorado Feed & Grain. Before that, appetizers in Des Moines consisted of a choice of tomato juice, fruit cocktail or shrimp cocktail."

Formaro concurred. "Before that, there wasn't a fried mushroom to be had on an

This wooden nickel promoted Colorado Feed and Grain, which Paul Trostel opened at 1925 Ingersoll Avenue in 1974. The restaurant became the local watering hole for many young professionals in Des Moines. *Author's collection.*

appetizer menu. Food definitely became more interesting in Des Moines by the 1980s, as local culinary innovators like Mike LaValle and Guido Fenu showed what was possible."

Other new flavors also entered Des Moines's dining scene around this time, thanks to an influx of legal immigrants. Iowa governor Robert D. Ray courageously welcomed hundreds of Tai Dam refugees to Iowa in the 1970s when they fled their home country at the end of the Vietnam War. While other states refused to accept the Tai Dam, Iowa embraced them. "Governor Ray literally saved people's lives," said Dave Oman, Governor Ray's former chief of staff, during an interview with WHO TV 13 in Des Moines following the death of Governor Ray in July 2018. "They enriched our culture and made our state a little more diverse. The Tai Dam never forgot it, and a lot of Iowans feel it was one of the best moves Governor Ray ever made."

The ripple effect of this act of kindness would eventually expand culinary options in the city, as the Tai Dam opened restaurants and shared the exotic flavors of their homeland with their new community. "When Governor Ray welcomed refugees from Southeast Asia, that kicked Des Moines's culinary trends into a whole new world," Lisa LaValle said.

Prior to this, ethnic flavors hadn't ventured much beyond the Chinese American fare at King Ying Low and Mexican flavors from Raul's Mexican Restaurant and Tasty Tacos. Founded in 1961 by Richard and Antonia Mosqueda, Tasty Tacos has become a Des Moines institution. These restaurateurs found success by taking their ethnic food, adding their own spin and making it mainstream in Iowa, LaValle noted.

Another factor reshaping dining in Des Moines was the Culinary Arts program at the Iowa Culinary Institute® at Des Moines Area Community College in Ankeny. "When I was in culinary school, you studied classical French cuisine if you wanted to be a chef," said Formaro, a 1986 East High School graduate and a second-generation Italian American whose parents came from Sicily and Calabria in Southern Italy. "Italian cooking, for example, wasn't a focus. Things have changed so much since then."

CHEERS TO THE CRAFT BEER REVOLUTION

One of those changes involved craft beer brewing. In the late 1980s and early 1990s, craft beer began to cross over from homebrewing hobbyists to the mainstream. In Des Moines, this momentum gained steam with the Raccoon River Brewing Company, which played a starring role in the development of the Tenth Street/Western Gateway area.

The popular restaurant, microbrewery and billiards hall opened in May 1997 at 200 Tenth Street in the historic Clemens Building. When the Raccoon River Brewing Company opened, it was only the second such novelty in Des Moines, following close on the heels of the Court Avenue Brewing Company, noted the *Des Moines Register* on February 10, 2015.

The Raccoon River Brewing Company played a starring role in the development of the Tenth Street/Western Gateway area of Des Moines and led a microbrewery renaissance when it opened in 1997. *Author's collection.*

The idea was still a crazy new concept in Des Moines, which was more of a Bud Light/Busch Light town back then. Options like Bandit IPA, touted as Raccoon River Brewing Company's strongest and most highly hopped ale, pushed tastes pretty far from mainstream beers.

Opening the Raccoon River Brewing Company in "downtown's mostly uninteresting west end might have been even crazier," added the *Des Moines Register*, noting that the business predated the restoration of the area's Temple for Performing Arts in the early 2000s and the opening of the Pappajohn Sculpture Park in 2009. Still, the Raccoon River Brewing Company became the hottest ticket in town when it opened. Former Colorado governor John Hickenlooper, who sought the 2020 Democratic presidential nomination, helped developed the business in the 1990s.

The restaurant was also an instant success. It promoted how it took "pub fare" to a new culinary level, thanks to chefs who used fresh ingredients to create flavorful sandwiches, salads and entrées. All good things must end, however. The Raccoon River Brewing Company closed in 2015, just shy of eighteen years in business.

IT'S ALL ABOUT THE FOOD AT THE IOWA STATE FAIR

While restaurants and food fads have come and gone, there are some facets of dining in Des Moines that never seem to change—and that's just how people like it.

Consider the internationally acclaimed Iowa State Fair. As one of the oldest and largest agricultural and industrial expositions in the country, the Iowa State Fair annually attracts more than 1 million people from all over the world each August. It was the only fair listed in the *New York Times*' best-selling travel book *1,000 Places to See Before You Die.*

The first Iowa State Fair was held in the southeast Iowa town of Fairfield from October 25 to October 27, 1854. The fair moved to its permanent home on the east side of Des Moines in 1886 on a park-like, 450-acre setting. From the beginning, the heart and soul of the Iowa State Fair has been food—the making and eating of it.

Thousands of people flock to the famous Pork Tent at the Iowa State Fair each year to enjoy pork chops on a stick, complete pork meals and more. For many people, a trip to the Iowa State Fair isn't complete without a visit to the Cattlemen's Beef Quarters restaurant too. "We've fed about 1.6 million people since we started," recalled John Mortimer in a 2014 interview with *Farm News*. Mortimer, a retired cattle producer from Dallas Center, helped establish the Cattlemen's Beef Quarters in 1984.

So what's the secret to decades of success at the Iowa State Fair? Offering new menu items that appeal to fairgoers, Mortimer said, along

Along with pork chops on a stick, the Iowa State Fair includes the West Des Moines United Methodist Church's food stand, which has been serving hearty breakfasts, pies and more since 1949. *Author's collection.*

with tried-and-true favorites like Hot Beef Sundaes (mashed potatoes covered with roast beef and gravy and topped with melted cheddar cheese and a cherry tomato).

Still hungry? Don't miss the West Des Moines United Methodist Church's historic food stand near the livestock barns. This is the kind of place where it's perfectly normal to enjoy a slice of homemade apple pie before 10:00 a.m. On a sunny morning at the fair in 2017, a long line of people had gathered at the food stand around 8:30 a.m., waiting patiently for breakfast. "We've been incredibly busy, which is a great problem to have," said Courtney Chabot Dreyer, a seventeen-year member of the church who had been volunteering at the food stand for fifteen years.

The food stand has always been located in its current spot, ever since church members decided to sell food at the state fair starting in 1949. The famous food stand is the last vestige of the area known as Church Row, where a group of churches once hosted dining halls. In fact, the West Des Moines United Methodist Church's food stand is the last remaining Christian organization to run a food stand on the fairgrounds, making it the final legacy of a tradition of service that dates back to the very first Iowa State Fair in 1854.

And serve it has. While the West Des Moines United Methodist Church's food stand is famous for its biscuits and gravy, which has been on the menu since 1949, people also flock to the stand for pecan rolls, cinnamon rolls, hot breakfasts and some of the best coffee at the fairgrounds. Other guests stop by to try the food stand's new offerings each year, including Stew's Big Boy Breakfast. New in 2017, this hearty offering included scrambled eggs, hash browns, sausage, biscuits and gravy.

While the food stand has been an integral part of the state fair's culinary history for decades, it wasn't until the last few years that church members addressed one missing element: something on a stick. Since they didn't have food on a stick, they added prayer on a stick. In addition to taking prayers on a stick home with them, fairgoers can write their prayer requests on small cards at the food stand. "Every day of the fair we collect prayer requests," said Chabot Dreyer, whose sons also volunteer at the food stand. "We take these requests to the church every night, and our members pray about these needs."

Now that's a whole new twist on soul food, and it's an important mission for church members.

Connecting with others became more difficult in 2020, however, when the Iowa State Fair was canceled due to the COVID-19 pandemic.

Fortunately, Iowans could still chow down on some of their fair favorites, including corn dogs, cinnamon rolls, fried Oreo cookies, funnel cakes, gyros and more, for two weekends in late July and early August 2020. The Iowa State Fair's "Taste of the Fair" event at the fairgrounds served up state fair classics and even brought some new vendors into the mix. In addition, the fair celebrated National Chocolate Chip Cookie Day 2020 with buckets of famous Barksdale's Iowa State Fair cookies. From 6:00 a.m. to 6:00 p.m. on August 4, people could head out to the fairgrounds to order a bucket of Barksdale's cookies, which have been an Iowa State Fair classic since 1993.

CLASSIC RESTAURANTS CARRY ON DES MOINES TRADITIONS

The Iowa State Fair isn't the only place that mixes nostalgia with fun and food. So does the Drake Diner, with its vibrant neon lights, cool chrome and checkerboard floor tile pattern that make you feel like you're back in the 1950s. Located near Drake University at 1111 Twenty-Fifth Street, the Drake Diner is everything you'd expect a classic diner to be, from the hearty burgers and creamy milkshakes to the blue-plate specials and homemade pies that change daily.

When its doors opened in 1987, the diner was an immediate hit. Patrons waited for a table most nights. It was so successful that William C. Knapp, founder of Iowa Realty, built two more restaurants: the West End Diner in West Des Moines and the North End Diner on Merle Hay Road in Johnston, both of which have been closed for a number of years.

While the Drake Diner continues to serve guests daily, Des Moines will never forget November 29, 1992. The diner was filled with guests that Sunday evening following Thanksgiving. A line wound out the front door on that cool, drizzly night. Suddenly, a man wearing a hooded sweatshirt pushed past the crowd at the front of the restaurant. He grabbed a manager, Cara McGrane, twenty-five, by the neck. When she screamed, her shot her in the face. She died instantly.

Another manager, Tim Burnett, twenty-eight, had come in on his day off to decorate a Christmas tree at the restaurant. He sprinted to help McGrane. The gunman shot Burnett in the head, killing him instantly. The killer grabbed less than $500 from the cash register and fled as others ducked

With its vibrant neon lights and cool chrome, the Drake Diner near Drake University relives the 1950s. Since it opened in 1987, it has served classics like burgers, creamy milkshakes and homemade pie. *Author's collection.*

for cover, noted the article "Drake Diner Murders Terrified Des Moines," a retrospective that ran in the November 29, 2017 issue of the *Des Moines Register* on the twenty-fifth anniversary of the murders.

Inside the diner, blood pooled in front of the hostess desk. Outside, one of the most intense police dragnets in the capital's history began to unfold. Police arrested Joseph "Jo-Jo" White Jr. on December 5, 1992. He was convicted of two counts of first-degree murder in 1993 for killing McGrane and Burnett and was sent to prison. "Two people were executed in front of forty or fifty people—he put all those people at risk," said Tom Suk, who had worked as a *Des Moines Register* night police reporter. "It was a hell of a shocking crime."

The Drake Diner killings could have stopped all the positive things going on in the area and the city at the time, said Donald Adams, then Drake's vice-president of student life. "But as a community, good people came together and made sure that did not happen," he told the *Des Moines Register*.

A spirit of community has long defined many other classic restaurants that have served the Des Moines area for decades. Maxie's Restaurant and Lounge, located at 1311 Grand Avenue in West Des Moines, has been serving steaks, seafood, sandwiches, pasta, chicken and more in a comfortable environment since 1967. "We invite you to #MeetAtMaxies Monday through Saturday for lunch, dinner and drinks," notes the restaurant's website. "Maxie's is the perfect place to dine with family, friends, clients or business associates."

Other beloved Des Moines restaurants include Italian American favorites like Noah's Ark at 2400 Ingersoll Avenue, which has been serving its legendary pizza, homemade bread, prime steak, fresh seafood, coffee drinks and more since 1946. When namesake Noah Lacona founded his eatery, he helped bring Neapolitan pizza to Des Moines. He also created an institution that makes you feel like you're stepping back into a different era defined by a relaxed atmosphere, great conversation and memorable meals.

A taste of Italy can also be found at Riccelli's Italian Restaurant on Des Moines's south side at 3803 Indianola Avenue, as well as Christopher's at 2816 Beaver Avenue. On February 1, 1963, Joe and Red Giudicessi became the owners of a quaint restaurant in the Beaverdale neighborhood. Under their steady watch, Christopher's became known for its excellent Italian American cuisine, friendly staff and an atmosphere fitting of any occasion. "From a table for two to a banquet room for 110, no event is too small or big," notes the website for Christopher's. "Joe's tradition of welcoming every guest continues today as one of the trademarks of the restaurant."

Italian food and hospitality served by local families also defines Scornovacca's Ristorante (1930 Southeast Fourteenth Street), which has been a destination since 1973, and Tumea & Sons Restaurant (1501 Southeast First Street). People gather at both places to enjoy the outdoor bocce ball courts, along with Italian-inspired cuisine and beverages.

Don't forget Chuck's Restaurant (3610 Sixth Avenue), which has been a fixture of the Highland Park neighborhood on Des Moines's north side since 1956. "Our employees are what hold us together," said Emily (Anderson) Jones, a Des Moines native and 2001 Hoover High School graduate who has owned the restaurant for six years. "It's like a big family."

That includes Nancy Coleman, who has been making Chuck's famous pizza from scratch for thirty-four years. "We make our own sausage from Chuck's original recipe and sell about three hundred to four hundred pizzas in a busy week," noted Jones, whose pizza ovens date from 1956, when Chuck Bisignano opened the restaurant.

Noah's Ark, located at 2400 Ingersoll Avenue, has served Des Moines since 1946. It's known for its legendary pizza, pasta, fresh bread, prime steak, fresh seafood, coffee drinks and more. *Author's collection.*

Bisignano was the younger brother of famed downtown Des Moines restaurateur Alphonse "Babe" Bisignano. Around 1945, Chuck Bisignano opened Chuck's Place at Sixth Avenue and Mulberry Street. It later became the G.I. Joe Club, a key club. Under strict Iowa liquor laws, police raided the tavern several times from 1950 to 1953. Bisignano was fined $1,000 and served six months in jail for keeping liquor where beer was sold.

He opened Chuck's in 1956 and worked there daily until a year before he died in 1992. After his daughter Linda Bisignano began running the restaurant following Chuck's death, a new Chuck's tradition was started. A special Thanksgiving dinner has been offered at Chuck's Restaurant since 1992. In conjunction with Parks Community Thanksgiving Dinner Inc., thousands of meals have been prepared over the years by volunteers helping neighbors enjoy a traditional Thanksgiving dinner.

The dinner's history can be traced to 1983, when it was coordinated by the Capitol Hill Lutheran Church. As the event grew, Linda Bisignano offered her restaurant as the location for food preparation and distribution. Each dinner included turkey, ham, sweet potatoes, gravy, dressing, green

Left: Chuck's Restaurant (3610 Sixth Avenue) has been a fixture of the Highland Park neighborhood on Des Moines's north side for decades. Each week, the restaurant sells hundreds of pizzas, which are baked in pizza ovens dating from 1956, when Chuck Bisignano opened the restaurant. *Author's collection.*

Below: Established in 1947, Tursi's Latin King (2200 Hubbell Avenue) has been blessed with loyal employees and customers for generations. "We've only had two owners and three chefs during the restaurant's seventy-three-year history," said owner Bob Tursi. *Author's collection.*

beans, cranberry sauce, a roll and a piece of pie. The event has grown from about 100 dinners in 1984 to more than 3,800 meals in 2019. "It takes about 300 volunteers to make it all happen," said Jones, who noted that some meals are eaten at Chuck's, while others are packaged as carry-outs and some are delivered.

Serving the community has also defined Tursi's Latin King (2200 Hubbell Avenue) for decades. Established by Jim and Rose Pigneri in 1947, the restaurant has been owned and operated by Bob and Amy Tursi since they purchased the business in August 1983. Pigneri, as well as Bob Tursi's parents, hailed from Terravecchia, Italy, before immigrating to the United States. To this day, their Italian heritage shines through in the restaurant's signature dishes, including Chicken Spiedini with Amogio Sauce.

Bob Tursi's first experience in the restaurant business came at age sixteen, when he worked at the Crystal Tree Restaurant on Fleur Drive. "I'm full-blooded Italian, and my father instilled a good work ethic in me and the pride that goes with having a good family name," said Tursi, who purchased Latin King when he was twenty-one.

The Latin King uses high-quality ingredients, including dairy products produced by the family-owned Anderson Erickson Dairy, which is located right across the street from the restaurant and has served Des Moines since 1930.

The Latin King has won numerous awards, including "Best Italian Restaurant" multiple times in *Cityview*'s Best of Des Moines poll, along with "Best Family Restaurant" (in 2012, 2013, 2014 and 2019) in the *Cityview* poll. The Latin King has also received the Restaurateur of the Year Award from the Iowa Hospitality Association, in addition to being named "Best Restaurant for a Business Lunch" by the *Des Moines Business Record*. "People expect more from longtime restaurants like the Latin King," Bob Tursi said. "They expect better service and consistent food." The Latin King has been blessed with loyal employees who provide this consistency. "We've only had two owners and three chefs during the restaurant's seventy-three-year history," Tursi said in 2019.

This keeps customers coming back for more. "I love a good tradition, and this little one right here just might be my favorite," wrote Katie (Skinner) Cox, a Lake City, Iowa native and Latin King fan who is raising her family in the Des Moines area. Five years ago, Cox and her husband started taking their two young sons to Tursi's Latin King on a night in November to kick off the holiday season. "We take our time, enjoy our meal, laugh and tell stories and only have to remind our little boys not to burp too loudly a couple of times," wrote Cox on her Facebook social media page in 2019. "I would like to think this tradition will stand the test of time and that every year on a cold November night you will find our family huddled around a table at The Latin King."

Latin King Chicken Spiedini

8 single, boneless chicken breasts, cut into 1-inch cubes

Marinade for the Chicken
1 cup canola oil
½ cup dry white wine
¾ cup freshly squeezed lemon juice
10 cloves garlic, finely minced
2 tablespoons kosher salt

¾ cup dried breadcrumbs
¾ cup Parmesan cheese

Thread the chicken breast cubes onto skewers. Mix together canola oil, dry white wine, lemon juice, garlic and salt. Place skewers in a non-reactive container and pour the marinade over them. Let them marinate in the refrigerator overnight.

When you're ready to cook, mix the breadcrumbs and Parmesan cheese together in a 9-by-13-inch glass pan. Shake off excess marinade from the chicken and then roll the skewers in the breadcrumb mixture. Let them rest for at least 30 minutes or up to 1 hour. The coating may become wet, which is fine.

Cook over medium-high heat on a grill, turning often, until the chicken is completely cooked through and browned nicely. You may also bake them in an oven at 475 degrees Fahrenheit for about 15 minutes, turning the skewers once. Allow breadcrumbs to brown.

Drizzle the cooked chicken with Amogio Sauce, and serve. Serves 8.

Amogio Sauce

1 cup extra virgin olive oil
½ cup dry white wine
½ cup lemon juice
3 cloves garlic, chopped
2 tablespoons kosher salt
pinch of dried red pepper flakes
¼ cup finely chopped fresh basil

Mix all ingredients well until emulsified. Let mixture stand briefly to allow flavors to mingle. Drizzle over Chicken Spiedini. Toss remaining Amogio Sauce with pasta, if desired.

GEORGE THE CHILI KING DATES TO 1920

While some people gravitate toward Des Moines restaurants like the Latin King, others have enjoyed George the Chili King Drive-In (5722 Hickman Road) for years. George the Chili King has been in operation since it was founded in downtown Des Moines in 1920 by George Karaidos. It has been at its current location at the corner of Hickman and Merle Hay Roads since 1952.

The restaurant is known for its heaping ladles of thick, saucy chili served over Coney Island–style hot dogs. It's also known for its massive fried pork tenderloin sandwiches, all served in a compact, retro diner atmosphere. George S. Karaidos Jr. (North High School class of 1951) followed in his father's footsteps and ran the restaurant for sixty-two years before his death in October 2019.

According to Karaidos's obituary, his biggest thrill was being asked to appear on Guy Fieri's *Diners, Drive-Ins and Dives* television program on the Food Network in October 2014. He was also mentioned the book *The Life and Times of the Thunderbolt Kid*, where author Bill Bryson proclaimed George the Chili King to have the best junk food when he was growing up in Des Moines in the 1950s. "There's something to be said for classic places like George the Chili King that specialize in blue-collar culinary charm," said John Busbee, host of KFMG Radio's *Culture Buzz* show in Des Moines.

George the Chili King was founded downtown in 1920. The drive-in has been located near the corner of Hickman and Merle Hay Roads since 1952, serving up chili-topped coneys, massive fried pork tenderloins, shakes and more. *Author's collection.*

Don't forget B&B Grocery, Meat & Deli, Busbee added. Located at 2001 Southeast Sixth Street, B&B ("home of the killer sandwiches") has been family owned and operated since May 1922. Its famous Dad's Killer Sandwich consists of roast beef, turkey breast, smoked ham, corned beef, pepper cheese, Swiss cheese, American cheese, lettuce, tomatoes, kosher pickles, mustard, Miracle Whip and Tuscan Italian dressing on an Italian hoagie roll.

THE MACHINE SHED REMAINS DEDICATED TO THE AMERICAN FARMER

Lest anyone forget where all this good food comes from, the Machine Shed Restaurant in Urbandale proudly proclaims "Farming is Everyone's Bread and Butter."

The Iowa Machine Shed restaurant offers an authentic taste of Iowa farm cooking. Dedicated to the American farmer, the Urbandale restaurant serves hearty soups, pork and beef entrées, fresh-baked goods and a signature apple dumpling dessert. *Author's collection.*

Dedicated to the American farmer, the first Machine Shed Restaurant opened on the outskirts of Davenport, Iowa, in 1978, followed by the Urbandale restaurant near Living History Farms, which tells the amazing story of how Iowans transformed the fertile midwestern prairies into the most productive farmland in the world.

The Machine Shed Restaurant in Urbandale offers family-style dining, along with an authentic taste of Iowa farm cooking with Haybaler top sirloins, roast pork loin with country sage dressing, the restaurant's signature apple dumpling dessert and Applesauce Sweet Bread, a perennial favorite that's served family-style with other delicious breads.

The Machine Shed Applesauce Sweet Bread

3 cups all-purpose flour
1 ½ teaspoons baking soda
1 teaspoon salt

1 cup butter, softened
1 ½ cups sugar
3 eggs
¼ cup evaporated milk or milk
1 teaspoon vanilla
1 ½ cups applesauce
2 tablespoons cinnamon-sugar

Grease the bottom and ½ an inch up the sides of two 8x4x2-inch loaf pans; set aside. In a medium bowl combine flour, baking soda and salt. Set aside.

In a large mixing bowl, beat butter with an electric mixer on medium to high speed for 30 seconds. Add sugar; beat until well combined. Beat in eggs, milk and vanilla. Beat in applesauce. Beat in flour mix until combined.

Divide mixture between prepared pans. Sprinkle tops of each with cinnamon-sugar. Bake at 325 degrees for 60 minutes or until a toothpick inserted near the centers comes out clean. Cool in pans on a wire rack for 10 minutes. Remove from pans. Cool completely.

COVID-19 PANDEMIC OF 2020 HIT RESTAURANTS HARD

While running a successful restaurant is never easy, everything became infinitely more complicated when the COVID-19 pandemic erupted in the spring and summer of 2020. In mid-March 2020, Iowa governor Kim Reynolds issued a State of Public Health Disaster Emergency, effective at noon on March 17. According to the proclamation, all restaurants and bars were closed to the public. Carry-out or drive-throughs could stay open. Food delivery services were also allowed to continue.

"With daily life upended in Iowa and across the nation because of COVID-19, the Iowa Restaurant Association (IRA) is warning of the financial pain many businesses are facing," reported Local 5 WOI-DT, Channel 5, the ABC-affiliated television station serving the Des Moines market.

A March 26, 2020 news story from Local 5 noted that revenues from local bars and restaurants had dropped 84 percent thus far in March 2020 compared to the same time last year. "The picture is grim," said Jessica Dunker, president and CEO of the Iowa Restaurant Association, in a news release. "We knew the precautionary step that shuttered large portions of our industry in an effort to fight the spread of the coronavirus would be detrimental, but our initial numbers indicate that for as many as 20% of our operators, there may be no coming back."

An Iowa Restaurant Association study from this time showed that 82 percent of restaurants and bars had laid off employees or intended to lay people off. "In many ways, we're collapsing," Dunker said in an interview with Local 5. "For some, the many things that the state and federal governments are trying to roll out, they just can't come quickly enough."

She also noted that restaurants that were offering just carry-out were doing just a fraction of the sales they had before closing their restaurants to dine-in orders. "Sixty-five percent of restaurants are trying to offer some sort of carry-out or delivery, but only 6 percent of those surveyed are set up with a drive-through," Dunker said. "Turning a table service restaurant menu, kitchen, infrastructure, team and business model into a carry-out program is difficult to do overnight. Many of our restaurants are simply providing carry-out to the community as a public service. There is no profit for a restaurant that a week ago averaged $15,000 in sales and is now doing $2,400 per week in takeout."

The restaurant industry's average net profit in good times is 5 percent, so an operator selling $2,400 per week has a net profit of less than $100, Dunker added. "You don't keep a business long with those numbers."

Iowa's restaurant industry understands its important role in delivering meals to people, Dunker noted. Before the state's on-premise service restrictions were put in place, 51 percent of every dollar spent on food was spent in the restaurant industry.

By mid-June 2020, the Des Moines City Council had approved a "Dine Out Des Moines" initiative to help restaurants and bars amid the COVID-19 pandemic. It allowed bars and food service establishments to set up service areas outside of their establishments on sidewalks, in parking lots and on city streets.

By late July 2020, state guidelines on social distancing to help control the spread of COVID-19 required that restaurants and bars maintain a six-foot distance between groups. State officials emphasized that restaurants and bars that didn't comply with social distancing guidelines would be hit first with fines and then with the suspension or cancelation of their alcohol or food service licenses.

While the future of Des Moines's restaurants is unclear, due to the COVID-19 pandemic, one thing is certain. The effects of 2020 will be long-lasting.

SAVOR THE MEMORIES

It's clear that great restaurants can make a lasting impression, even long after the last meal is served. Whether you prefer the classic restaurants still in business in the Des Moines area or you miss your favorite lost restaurant, there's no doubt that food memories can trigger deeper emotions. The taste, aroma and texture of food can be extraordinarily evocative, bringing back memories of not only the meal but also the feelings associated with the place where it all happened.

"If you loved a certain restaurant, was it because they had the best food in town? Maybe not," Formaro said. "But the people you were with were the best, and that's what makes eating at your favorite restaurant so special."

Bibliography

Bisignano, Alphonse. *Cooking the Italian Way.* Minneapolis, MN: Lerner Publications Company, 2002.

Bone, Eugenia, and Julia della Croce. *Tasting Italy: A Culinary Journey.* Washington, D.C.: National Geographic, 2018.

Bryson, Bill. *The Life and Times of the Thunderbolt Kid.* New York: Broadway Books, 2006.

Cannon, Lou. *Governor Reagan: His Rise to Power.* New York: PublicAffairs, 2003.

Caufield, Rachel Paine. *The Iowa Caucus.* Charleston, SC: Arcadia Publishing, 2016.

Hobbins, Carmela Tursi. *Celebrations with Carmela's Cucina.* Minneapolis, MN: Nordin Press, 2011.

Ingham, Vicki. *Younkers: The Friendly Store.* Charleston, SC: The History Press, 2016.

McCoy Davis, Judy. *Greater Des Moines: Iowa's Commercial Center.* Memphis, TN: Towery Publishing Inc., 1999.

McCue, Craig S., and Ron Playle. *Des Moines.* Charleston, SC: Arcadia Publishing, 2007.

Mills, George. *Looking in Windows: Surprising Stories of Old Des Moines.* Ames: Iowa State University Press, 1991.

Offenburger, Chuck. *Babe: An Iowa Legend.* Ames: Iowa State University Press, 1989.

Parker, Honesty. *African Americans of Des Moines and Polk County*. Charleston, SC: Arcadia Publishing, 2011.

Silag, Bill. *Outside In: African-American History in Iowa, 1838–2000*. Des Moines: State Historical Society of Iowa, 2001.

Whitaker, Jan. *Tea at the Blue Lantern Inn: A Social History of the Tea Room Craze in America*. New York: St. Martin's Press, 2002.

About the Author

If you enjoy fascinating, true stories well told, you have a lot in common with Darcy Dougherty Maulsby, Iowa's Storyteller. Maulsby is proud to be part of a family that operates a Century Farm in Calhoun County, Iowa, near Lake City and Yetter. She also runs her own marketing/communications company, Darcy Maulsby & Company. She helps businesses discover and share their "wow" stories. Capturing this magic helps inspire people to dream bigger, revitalize their businesses and communities and change the world for the good, one story at a time.

An award-winning author, Maulsby has published four books of nonfiction Iowa history, including *Iowa Agriculture: A History of Farming, Food and Family*; *A Culinary History of Iowa: Sweet Corn, Pork Tenderloins, Maid-Rites and More*; *Calhoun County*; and *Dallas County*. Maulsby is a popular speaker who has addressed thousands of people across Iowa and beyond at libraries, schools, museums, 4-H clubs, FFA chapters, civic groups, fairs and other events. She has been featured on the Travel Channel, the INSP television network, Iowa PBS, Iowa Public Radio, WHO 1040 Radio, *USA Today* and other media outlets.

Maulsby is a past president and current director with the Calhoun County Farm Bureau, president of the Calhoun County Corn Growers and District Advisory Committee member for the Iowa Soybean Association. She also serves on the Calhoun County Historic Preservation Commission and is the president of the board of Central School Preservation in Lake City. This award-winning home cook has earned blue ribbons for her mixed-berry jam at the Iowa State Fair and her molasses cookies at the Clay County Fair, dubbed the "The World's Greatest County Fair." She enjoys reading, cooking, going for Sunday drives in the country, helping her family on the farm and laughing at the antics of her beloved pets, including Maggie the Red Heeler and Lieutenant Dan the Cat. Visit her online at www.darcymaulsby.com.